The American Education Policy Landscape

In today's complex educational environment, it's critical for educators to understand the policy landscape. Research-based and grounded in a non-ideological perspective, *The American Education Policy Landscape* is an essential guide for educators, graduate students, and policymakers alike. This accessible resource unpacks complex concepts and provides a comprehensive overview of early childhood, K–12, and higher education policy issues, including governance structures at the local, state, and national levels; the process of policymaking; issues of educational finance; and the impact of stakeholders. *The American Education Policy Landscape* provides aspiring and practicing educators, analysts, researchers, and policymakers with the foundational knowledge and context for understanding education policy, thereby enabling them to make effective decisions, provide informed advice, and craft critical research questions on education.

Jennifer A. Rippner, Ph.D., J.D., is Executive Director for Policy and Partnerships for the University System of Georgia and the Coordinator for the state of Georgia's P–20 Council, the Alliance of Education Agency Heads (AEAH).

The American Education Policy Landscape

Jennifer A. Rippner

Routledge
Taylor & Francis Group

NEW YORK AND LONDON

First published 2016
by Routledge
711 Third Avenue, New York, NY 10017

and by Routledge
2 Park Square, Milton Park, Abingdon, Oxon, OX14 4RN

Routledge is an imprint of the Taylor & Francis Group, an informa business

© 2016 Taylor & Francis

The right of Jennifer A. Rippner to be identified as author of this work
has been asserted by her in accordance with sections 77 and 78 of the
Copyright, Designs and Patents Act 1988.

Library of Congress Cataloging-in-Publication Data
A catalog record for this book has been requested

ISBN: 978-1-138-84519-0 (hbk)
ISBN: 978-1-138-84520-6 (pbk)
ISBN: 978-1-315-72824-7 (ebk)

Typeset in Bembo
by Apex CoVantage, LLC

Printed and bound in the United States of America by Publishers Graphics,
LLC on sustainably sourced paper.

This book is dedicated to the sincere and inspired professionals working to affect educational policy every day on behalf of America's students.

Contents

Preface

This book is a culmination of 20 years of study and experiences within America's education policy landscape. What could be characterized as a rather disparate collection of personal and professional interests has turned out to be a very useful self-directed course of study in education policy that has provided me a unique viewpoint. It is my desire to share this view with a wider audience in order to offer a broad perspective on America's educational system—one that those of us so deeply entrenched in education policy hardly ever take. This perspective is increasingly important as our local, state, and national goals span the early childhood through postsecondary, or P–20, education pipeline. For example, achieving 100% student reading proficiency by third grade depends on what happens before kindergarten, and college completion rates depend on what happens during secondary education, if not before.

Although education governance continues to occur in sectors (early childhood, K–12, higher education), an understanding of other sectors and coordination between them is needed. This was made very clear during my variety of experiences. As a governor's education advisor, I had a fair amount of influence on state education policy. However, like many of my peers around the country, I was young and relatively inexperienced, thrown into a world where it is easy to believe that ideology is policy. A resource such as this book would have helped me to make more informed analyses and recommendations. Later, as the leader of a state agency responsible for early learning through higher education accountability, I could start to see the systemic connections between the sectors through various research projects we conducted. For example, the high school a student attended had a great influence on whether and where a student went to college. After my state service, I worked as a senior policy advisor for a national law firm based in Washington, DC. I had the opportunity to work on early learning, K–12, and higher education policy projects at national and federal levels with major foundations, government agencies, associations, and policy institutes. I observed firsthand how policy is shaped and communicated at that level. Most policymakers and staff at the local and state levels do not get this type of view, and hopefully they can benefit from my experiences and assessments. Finally, my training as a researcher has illuminated the ways policy and practice can benefit from research and how the connection between research and policy occurs too infrequently. All too often, researchers write for other researchers, and policymakers don't understand or know where to find relevant research. As one researcher humorously notes, it may be that policy scholars are from Venus and policymakers are from Mars (Birnbaum, 2000).

The variety of these experiences has convinced me that greater numbers of education policy leaders with broader bases of knowledge about the education pipeline may improve our field. Therefore, this book will provide readers with the pertinent context for understanding and developing early childhood through higher education policy in the United States. There is no existing single resource for those interested in education policy to understand the current education policymaking environment, which is especially important to those who make policy (as leaders or staff), implement policy (as administrators or educators), or research policy (as academics or students). Through a politically neutral, research-based viewpoint, I provide an overview of early childhood, K–12, and higher education policy issues; education governance structures at the local, state, and national levels; finance mechanisms; and the process of policymaking (including the role of relevant stakeholders and interpreting research).

Intended Audience

Educational policymakers, staff, academics, and graduate students will benefit from reading this book by gaining a foundation of knowledge for understanding the American educational system as a whole in order to better their abilities to make decisions, provide advice, and craft research questions on education. The book will not give the reader a silver bullet for improving educational outcomes, but it will provide a unique view by asking: What are the main components of America's educational system, and how do they connect (or not, as the case may be)? How do the nation's collective educational goals fit with the existing system?

Organization of the Book

This book is comprised of three parts. Part I provides an overview of the American education system and educational policy; Part II addresses the three sectors (early childhood education, K–12, higher education); and Part III discusses tools for continued learning. The first chapter provides the necessary background for understanding the American education system and educational policy. This chapter attempts to make the case for greater understanding and collaboration across sectors, and it clarifies the intent of the book—namely to provide a foundation of information for educators, policymakers, staff, and researchers. Chapter 2 will focus on the structure of the American system of education, starting with a brief section on the historical and legal development of the system, including the founders' (sometimes competing) visions for public education. Knowledge about the emergence of separate governance structures for early childhood education, K–12, and higher education will help readers understand how the U.S. came to have its modern education structure. The modern structure will then be detailed, including the respective roles of local, state, and federal governments and, within those levels, the various major influences on education policy such as governors, legislatures, boards of education, and interest groups. Chapter 3 will provide basic information on the policymaking process. Because the focus of the book is educational policy, it is important to not only understand the structure of the system and its stakeholders, but also to understand *how* policy is made. A variety of policymaking theories will be presented in order to shed light on why certain things happen the way they do and how/why certain policy outcomes occur. For example, Berry and Berry's (2007) theory of policy diffusion helps to explain how specific policies spread across organizations and geographic regions (e.g., state to state). A basic understanding of policymaking theory can help policymakers and other stakeholders place their decisions and actions in a larger and more predictable context.

The second part of this book will provide detailed information on the three main educational sectors: early childhood education, K–12, and higher education. The organization of Chapters 4, 5, and 6 will be similar, with each detailing the following aspects of each sector: governance, finance, major stakeholders, and major policy issues. The governance section of each of these chapters focuses on the local, state, and federal roles in the sector, as applicable. It sometimes veers into the programmatic aspects of the governance role. For example, in Chapter 4, I explore the federal government's role in early childhood education and then segue into a discussion of its Head Start program. I selected policy issues within each sector that are topping policy debate agendas and affect a large segment of students or the profession. Inevitably, this leaves out many worthwhile topics, such as policies related to English language learners and class size debates. Overall, the aim of the policy sections is to provide the reader with a broad base of knowledge and context for further examination and study.

Finally, the third part of this book will provide readers with tools that will help them continue to grow their knowledge bases and seek ways to understand and collaborate with other sectors. Chapter 7 will provide readers with an introduction to research interpretation and utilization. It is vitally important for those involved in developing education policy to understand the variety of and differences between sources of research; for example, information gleaned from scholarly research journals can be very different from that contained in think-tank white papers. It will also discuss the latest evidence on how policymakers utilize research in the policy process. The final chapter concludes the book with thoughts on the future of P–20 education governance, including new possibilities inherent in statewide longitudinal data systems and use of P–20 councils to bridge the sector divides.

Notes on Format

While the book's intent is to be accessible to anyone with an interest in education policy, there are many research citations throughout. This is not meant to overwhelm the reader or to seem overly scholarly, but to be transparent about the sources used to inform this book. Along with the suggestions for further research, these citations can be used as springboards for more intense study on a certain topic.

Further, as noted previously, I aim to have a politically neutral and research-based viewpoint throughout the book. There are two potential limitations to this. First, everyone has inherent biases and a unique worldview, and as much as I strive to be objective, those probably come through. Second, I have had experiences, such as serving a Republican governor and being involved with charter school policy, that could indicate that I am of a certain political persuasion. I'm not. I believe in sound, well-executed policies and am usually centrist in my views. I also continue to toggle between the research and policy worlds, never really feeling like I completely fit in either. My ideal world is one dominated by non-ideological, evidence-based, or at least common-sense-based, policies. My aim is to make this book a balance of those worlds and present information as an honest broker.

Generally, I present data as a whole (national or state averages) and by student subgroup (e.g., gender, race, ethnicity, family income). Student subgroup data often provide an indication of how the American value of equality of opportunity is playing out in our educational system. Generally, educational achievement and attainment have increased for all student subgroups over time, but gaps remain between groups. Hence, many policymakers are interested in addressing the "achievement gap" when considering education policies. Recently, some policymakers and education advocates have placed an increased focus on gaps between students from varying levels of family income, potentially signaling an increasing disparity between the "haves" and the "have nots." While the effect of student socioeconomic status on educational achievement is not the focus of this book, it is important to mention because many education policy priorities discussed in the forthcoming chapters try to address it. An excellent resource for an in-depth exploration of the issue is the recent book *Our Kids: The American Dream in Crisis* by scholar Robert D. Putnam (2015).

It is my hope that this book on the American education policy landscape is a starting point of conversation and study for educators, policymakers, analysts, and researchers interested in supporting more effective and efficient educational policies. Understanding how the system works and how policies are developed should provide a suitable jumping off point for readers' greater exploration into more specific aspects of the American educational policy process.

References

Berry, F., & Berry, W. (2007). Innovation and diffusion models in policy research. In P. Sabatier (Ed.), *Theories of the Policy Process* 2nd *Edition* (pp. 223–260). Boulder, CO: Westview Press.

Birnbaum, R. (2000). Policy scholars are from Venus; policy makers are from Mars. *The Review of Higher Education, 23*(2), 119–132.

Putnam, R. (2015). *Our kids: The American dream in crisis.* New York, NY: Simon & Schuster.

Acknowledgments

The generosities of many have helped inspire and execute this book. First, I want to acknowledge those who gave me an opportunity to serve in impactful education policy positions, namely Dr. Ellen West, former principal of Loften Educational Center in Gainesville, Florida, and former Georgia governor Sonny Perdue. The mentorship of these two individuals inspired and challenged me to dream big and act big.

I appreciate my fellow education policy "wonks" who have challenged and encouraged me through our ongoing education policy discussions. These include Holly Green, Erin Hames, Lauren Holcomb, Bonnie Holliday, Teresa MacCartney, Christy McGill, Debbie Pepin, Angela Recker, Amy Starzynski, and Judson Turner. Last, but not least, it was Hannah Heck who said it was always "education, education, education" with me, and she was right!

I was fortunate to have several academic mentors at the University of Georgia's Institute of Higher Education, where I earned my Ph.D. and served as a postdoctoral research and teaching associate. These include my advisor, Jim Hearn, as well as Libby Morris, Chuck Knapp, Erik Ness, and Rob Toutkoushian. John Dayton and Elizabeth DeBray of the University of Georgia's College of Education have also been very influential in my work. I appreciate the support of the Institute and the University of Georgia for providing a professional home while I wrote this book.

Finally, no great endeavor is ever accomplished without the emotional support of others. Whether readers ultimately judge the book as good or poor, the writing of it was indeed a great endeavor. I am so thankful for those who have encouraged me along the way. Barbara and Charles Whitfield helped me understand that I had something important to say. Mary Berkson, Donny Rippner, and Barry Berkson continually inspire me with their unyielding passion in the classroom. My mother, Mary Berkson, has perhaps been my biggest lifelong cheerleader, always making me feel like I am contributing something important to the world. Last, but not least, I am deeply grateful for my husband Jeff Ezell's unyielding support as I wrote this book. Not only is he the kindest, most generous man I know, but he also cooks as well as my mother.

Chapter 1

Introduction

If you stood close to a mosaic, you would see individual stones or gems, but the full picture wouldn't emerge until you took a step back. To see the whole picture requires a change of perspective.

Tom Shadyac, film producer/author

Education as a System

When you or I visit a doctor for a physical, we are examined from head to toe. In fact, we may find it a bit odd if the doctor examined only our legs one year and our arms in another year in order to assess our overall health. Doctors recognize that our bodies are sets of interrelated systems that need to be examined and understood as a whole. Even if we see specialized doctors (such as those for dermatology, endocrinology, or neurology), we still have general practitioners that assess our overall health. Further, although doctors often specialize in one area, they share the same basic foundation of medical training because their specialties exist within the same context as other specialties.

Education in the United States can be viewed in much the same way—as a set of interrelated systems. However, education lacks the overview needed to assess, diagnose, and treat its overall health. Since the country's founding, education has been developed, administered, and analyzed in distinct sectors (early childhood education, K–12, higher education). Today, there are separate agencies, boards, legislative committees, accountability mechanisms, and funding streams for each sector at the local, state, and national levels that institutionalize the disconnected nature of the system as a whole. Those who make policies related to education rarely seek out or have access to the big picture.

The disjointed nature of the educational system is reinforced through the programs that prepare professionals to work in the system. Graduate-level education programs prepare professionals and researchers to work in or study one (versus all) of the sectors. Often, education policy and research analysts earn degrees in fields other than education, such as public administration or political science. In any of these programs, there is rarely an overview course or experience that gives budding education policy analysts and researchers an overview of the P–20[1] system.

As with any system that affects a core social value and has a good deal of funding associated with it, education has its share of related interest groups. These associations, lobbyists, consultants, and think tanks usually specialize in one sector as well. This specialization often results in reports and articles focused on very specific education issues. There is rarely big or deep thinking on the overall educational system and proposed solutions for a better way.

While all of this specialization makes sense as the American education system grows larger and more complex, we must not forget the value in understanding the sum of its parts. An understanding of the whole may provide greater clarity on the problems that plague the individual parts, as well as the interactions between them.

Problems Related to Educational Achievement

Perceived problems with public education are long-standing and systemic. Dissatisfaction with educational achievement and attainment permeates the history of education in the United States. As early as 1830, a group of American thought leaders gathered to discuss education and "concluded that the level of learning in America was not high enough" (Whitehead, 1973, p. 104). Since then, policy leaders have continued to bemoan the state of education as evidenced in the 1893 Committee of Ten Report, the 1983 Nation at Risk report, and the 2001 No Child Left Behind federal legislation. Today the focus is on college-level attainment, as the United States has seen its preeminence in the percentage of adults with a higher education credential decline. In 1995, the U.S. ranked second in college attainment among 19 countries with comparable data, and in 2013, the U.S. ranked 11th among similar countries (Organisation for Economic Co-operation and Development, 2014). The Organisation for Economic Co-operation and Development (OECD) (2014) found that while the U.S. improved its overall postsecondary attainment rate of 25- to 34-year-olds to 45%, other countries improved at greater rates. An adviser to the OECD claims that the U.S. is "the only country in the industrialised world in which the generation entering the workforce does not have higher college attainment levels than the generation about to leave the workforce" (Schleicher, 2012, p. 1).

Given its potential impact on the economy, these statistics have caught the interest of our national and state leaders. In 2009, President Obama set a nationwide goal for 60% of U.S. citizens to attain a college credential by 2020 so the U.S. can regain its position of leadership among developed countries (The White House, 2009). The U.S. is far from meeting that goal. Recent data show that 37.7% of persons aged 25 and older in the U.S. have at least an associate's degree (National Center for Education Statistics, 2015). Pulling the U.S. even further from the goal is the disparity in educational attainment between races and ethnicities. Minorities represent the fastest growing populations in the U.S., but proportionally, their postsecondary attainment is lower (Carnevale & Strohl, 2013; Nunez & Oliva, 2009; U.S. Census Bureau, 2013). Almost 59% of Asians, 42% of Whites, 27% of Blacks, and 20% of Hispanics aged 25 or older have at least an associate's degree (National Center for Education Statistics, 2015). Not only are there disparities in attainment between races, but students of different races are receiving different educations. "Whites have captured most of the enrollment growth at the 468 most selective and well-funded four-year colleges, while African Americans and Hispanics have captured most of the enrollment growth at the increasingly overcrowded and under-resourced open-access two- and four-year colleges" (Carnevale & Strohl, 2013, p. 6).

Educational leaders and policymakers must focus on *all* students achieving at high levels in order to meet national educational attainment goals. Part of the issue is that high school graduates are ill-prepared for college-level work. Between 28% and 40% of all first-time undergraduates at four-year colleges take at least one remediation class (National Conference of State Legislatures, 2013). This increases to over 50% at two-year colleges (National Conference of State Legislatures, 2013). Therefore, it is not surprising that only 60% of those entering a bachelor's degree program complete it within eight years, and only 18% of students entering an associate's degree program complete within four years (Complete College America, 2011). The figures are even worse when considering part-time students (Complete College America, 2011). Clearly, something must be done differently to meet our national goals. Nancy Zimpher, chancellor of the State University of New York, writes: "This leaking educational pipeline is at the core of all our challenges. As a nation, we have yet to connect the dots between the various stages of a student's education" (2013, p. 40).

The Need for a Broad View

Our current educational goals require a more holistic view of the educational pipeline and its related systems. Policymakers and professionals in each sector need to be able to peer over the ledges of their silos and see how what they (or the boards on which they sit) are doing affects students and policy in earlier and later years. For example, a state higher education governing board decision about college entry requirements affects high school curriculum. A local board of education's decision to scale back district arts programs in order to focus on math education may conflict with a recent ramp-up of arts education offerings at the local community college.

But, this doesn't happen. Policymakers, education policy analysts, and researchers dive deeply into their own sectors and rarely rise up to see the bigger picture. Some leaders, namely the president of the United States and our states' governors, have a great imperative to do this. They are responsible for the entire educational system of their respective polities. Yet, very few analysts are prepared to advise or inform these leaders on overarching educational policy issues, given the segmented and siloed nature of existing avenues for training education policy specialists as described previously. Imagine if a new cadre of policy professionals and researchers was viewing educational systems at a coordinated level. Perhaps some of our more intractable educational problems, such as increasing college success for underserved populations or increasing third grade students' reading levels, would be easier to remedy because people are looking at the entire educational pipeline.

For those who are new to education policymaking, such as new local and state education board members, understanding the landscape is daunting when faced with a multitude of immediate and important decisions. This really hit home during a state commission retreat where one of my fellow commissioners, who is an experienced and successful businessman, asked "how do I learn about education?" The truth is, I did not know how to answer him. Where does one get a fact-based, viewpoint-neutral (at least in *aim*) overview of the American education system? We certainly are not lacking in materials to read, but most focus on one sector, and even then, they focus on a specific aspect of the sector (for example, governance, funding, or curriculum). Further, most works on education—whether books, white papers, or blog posts—provide a certain point of view, such as the exorbitant cost of higher education or the lack of preparedness of school leaders. These points of view may be true and are important to discuss, but the field is lacking a viewpoint-neutral overview of the entire system—one that I argue is greatly needed to meet our overarching educational goals and, hence, is the purpose of this book.

The Need for Collaboration

Beyond the need for greater cross-sector understanding, there is a need for collaboration between the sectors. In the 1990s, states began creating councils that brought together various combinations of education stakeholders to discuss overarching P–20 issues. The thinking was that if states needed more students to be prepared for secondary and postsecondary work, the state education sectors must communicate and collaborate. The councils spread quickly, and by 2008, 38 states had some sort of council (Education Commission of the States, 2008). Collaboration across sectors is even more important today because national and state goals center on student readiness for and success in each level of education. This necessitates not only understanding, but also partnerships between early childhood, K–12, and higher education entities to ensure students are prepared for the next level of learning.

Some have theorized that full implementation of common student learning standards and assessments will effectively bridge the divide. Streamlined articulation between sectors is only one piece of the puzzle, however. Inevitably, new legislation appears, workforce needs evolve, and state and local leaders change, which requires continuous coordination. Sustained collaboration is necessary for a continuously strong education pipeline.

Numerous observers see the promise in collaboration. An analysis of 2014 gubernatorial state of the state addresses by the American Association of State Colleges and Universities (2014) found that a key theme was the need for stronger alignment between K–12 and college or career. Further, over the past 20 years, various groups such as Achieve, Inc., the Education Trust, the National Association of System Heads, and College Board have brought together state K–12 and higher education teams to work on such issues as defining college and career readiness, creating articulation agreements, and implementing common standards. Yet, this collaboration is usually not sustained after the meeting or institute is concluded. Agency leaders have a lot on their plates, and anything that does not demand immediate attention is often a low priority. This is why state P–20 councils make sense. A regular forum for collaboration between state education sectors could only result in streamlined policies and programs, right? Wrong. Although states have been tinkering with these councils for decades, many states have disbanded the effort, reorganized the council, and/or continue to meet with few or no results.

There are currently 22 active state councils, and they take many different forms (Rippner, 2014). Some include stakeholders outside of government, while others remain very small, including only state agency leaders. Often the governor leads the council.

Because there is no widely accepted definition of council effectiveness, it is difficult to assess these structures. Still, most research papers and policy briefs find some benefit to these councils and often provide recommendations for implementation based on often-noted "barriers to success." Recent research has found that "successful" P–20 councils "build trust" and "maintain communications" between stakeholders, have adequate support for the council through staffing and funding, and have connected data systems

(Nunez & Oliva, 2009). It is important that such qualities lead to meaningful results. However, other research from the National Center for Public Policy and Higher Education found that P–20 councils often spend too much time discussing and planning initiatives and too little time translating those activities into action (Shulock, 2009). Greater discussion about P–20 councils and collaboration between the sectors will occur in Chapter 8.

Many state leaders seem to understand the need for collaboration, and very often they are passionate about making it happen. At the same time, uncertainties remain regarding the most effective mechanism for fostering collaboration. Who should be at the table? Who should lead the group? What should be on the agenda? How should the work get done? All of these questions must be answered, and it is not as easy as defining a singular "best practice," because each state has a unique education governance structure as well as political and policy contexts.

The disconnection between educational levels is rather unique to the American education system. One observer claims, "American K–12 and higher education systems are among the world's least-linked education structures" (Boswell, 2000, p. 4). This argument is not new. In 1909, the Carnegie Foundation described the American system of education as a system of disparate institutions without any linkage or coordination (VanOverbeke, 2008). Other developed countries have established more structural connections between secondary and postsecondary education, but these connections come with some trade-offs. America's system of education is largely driven by ideals of equality of opportunity—that all students should have access to a high-quality K–12 education no matter where they live or what their circumstances. The notion of equality has only grown over time. In international comparisons between the U.S. and other developed countries' systems of education, the American system is decidedly "untracked," meaning students are not placed into certain courses of study that prepare them for predetermined outcomes (e.g., college or a trade). In 1985, with three general "tracks" in comprehensive high schools (e.g., academic, vocational, and general), the U.S. was an outlier from other countries that instituted strict tracks as early as primary school (Clark, 1985). The case against tracking in the United States has only grown throughout the 21st century. Now, all students in most comprehensive high schools are working toward college and career readiness, with the standards for each often being nearly identical because most new jobs require advanced skills.

Eventually, tracking does appear in the American educational system, but it happens much later than in other countries. The American higher educational system is differentiated and competitive (Clark, 1985). Americans have tolerated this type of stratification after high school, given that, theoretically, all students have an equal chance to apply and be accepted to any institution of higher learning if they meet the qualifications. However, there is increasing consternation with this system's results as lower proportions of low-income and/or ethnic students attend college, and when they do attend, disproportionate numbers of these groups attend less-selective institutions than wealthy and/or White students. This has generated a redoubling of efforts to bridge secondary and postsecondary sectors to ensure more students of all backgrounds are prepared to attend and succeed in college.

As discussed in Chapter 6, college enrollment numbers across all groups are rising, but not as fast as leaders hope, and gaps in achievement are apparent throughout the education pipeline. Perhaps rather than having experts at each educational level continue to toil in shoring up their portions of the educational pipeline, it would make sense to focus on the connection points in the pipeline. Maybe this will give us the boost in achievement and equity that we seek. Focusing on connections starts with education policy professionals sharing a common field of knowledge about the pipeline.

Note

1. P–20 education is commonly used shorthand to refer to the entirety of a student's potential education career—from pre-kindergarten (pre-K) to graduate school (year 20). Although educational endeavors can begin prior to pre-K and extend beyond graduate school, P–20 will be the term used throughout this book to refer to the education pipeline.

References

American Association of State Colleges and Universities. (2014, March 11). *The 2014 gubernatorial state of the state addresses and higher education*. Retrieved from www.aascu.org/policy/state-policy/2014StateoftheStateAddresses.pdf

Boswell, K. (2000). Building bridges or barriers? Public policies that facilitate or impede linkages between community colleges and local school districts. *New Directions for Community Colleges, 111*, 3–15.

Carnevale, A., & Strohl, J. (2013). *Separate & unequal: How higher education reinforces the intergenerational reproduction of white racial privilege—executive summary.* Retrieved from https://cew.georgetown.edu/report/separate-unequal/

Clark, B. (1985). Conclusions. In B. Clark (Ed.), *The school and the university: An international perspective* (pp. 290–325). Berkeley: University of California Press.

Complete College America. (2011). *Time is the enemy.* Retrieved from www.completecollege.org/docs/Time_Is_the_Enemy.pdf

Education Commission of the States. (2008). *P–16/P–20 database.* Retrieved from www.ecs.org/

National Center for Education Statistics, U.S. Department of Education. (2015). Percentage of persons 18 to 24 years old and 25 and over, by educational attainment, race/ethnicity, and selected subgroups: 2008 and 2013. In *Digest of education statistics 2013 (chap. 1).* Retrieved from https://nces.ed.gov/programs/digest/d14/tables/dt14_104.40.asp?current=yes

National Conference of State Legislatures. (2013, February). *Reforming remedial education.* Retrieved from www.ncsl.org/issues-research/educ/improving-college-completion-reforming-remedial.aspx

Nunez, A., & Oliva, M. (2009). Organizational collaboration to promote college access: A P–20 framework. *Journal of Hispanic Higher Education, 8*(4), 322–339.

Organisation for Economic Co-operation and Development. (2014, September). *Education at a glance 2014 interim report: OECD indicators.* Retrieved from www.oecd.org/edu/eag-interim-report.htm

Rippner, J. (2014). State P–20 councils and collaboration between K–12 and higher education. *Educational Policy.* Advance online publication. doi:10.1177/0895904814558008

Schleicher, A. (2012, December 10). *U.S. education is getting left behind.* Retrieved from www.huffingtonpost.com/andreas-schleicher/us-education_b_2268873.html

Shulock, N. (2009). From dialogue to policy? A comparison of P-16 councils in three states. In *States, schools, and colleges: Policies to improve student readiness for college and strengthen coordination between schools and colleges* (pp. 133–139). Washington, DC: The National Center for Public Policy and Higher Education.

U.S. Census Bureau. (2013, June 13). *Asians fastest growing race or ethnic group in 2012, Census Bureau reports.* Retrieved from www.census.gov/newsroom/press-releases/2013/cb13–112.html

VanOverbeke, M. (2008). *The standardization of American schooling: Linking secondary and higher education, 1870–1910.* New York, NY: Palgrave.

Whitehead, J.S. (1973). *The separation of college and state.* New Haven, CT: Yale University Press.

The White House. (2009, July 14). *Excerpts from the President's remarks in Warren, Michigan and fact sheet of the American Graduation Initiative.* Retrieved from www.whitehouse.gov/the-press-office/excerpts-presidents-remarks-warren-michigan-and-fact-sheet-american-graduation-init

Zimpher, N. (2013). Systemness: Unpacking the value of higher education systems. In J. Lane & B. Johnstone (Eds.), *Higher education systems 3.0—Harnessing systemness, delivering performance* (pp. 27–44). New York, NY: SUNY Press.

Part I

OVERVIEW OF THE AMERICAN EDUCATION SYSTEM

Chapter 2

The Structure of the American Education System

Introduction

The purpose of this chapter is to provide a brief synopsis of the American education governance structure and examine how it was shaped to its current form. If we accept McGuinn and Manna's (2013) definition of policy as "the array of initiatives, programs, laws, regulations, and rules that the governance system chooses to produce" (p. 9), we see how important education governance systems are to educational policymaking and how important it is that students of education policy understand the complicated structure.

The Evolution of Separate Systems

The historical origins of both secondary and postsecondary education have their roots in the early American settlers' familiarity with England's system of education (Bailyn, 1960). In England, the large, extended families took responsibility for a child's education. There was not a clear boundary where the family ended and society began, so distinctly separate primary educational institutions were not common. When children reached a certain age, they began an apprenticeship to learn a trade. Children of the elite matriculated to universities to study rhetoric, classical languages, and other subjects that gave a foundation of cultural knowledge. Knowledge for its own sake was prized, but these institutions also produced leaders who could serve the community such as clergy, teachers, and politicians (Bailyn, 1960).

Although this is what early settlers were familiar with, this system was not easily transmitted to the new colonies because practical considerations outweighed cultural ones (Bailyn, 1960). American settlers were busy starting towns and businesses and providing for their families. Education had to further those aims. The family unit was not as vast or strong as in England. The hardships of colonial life resulted in smaller families that were more distinct from the communities in which they lived, often with the children being more adaptable to and comfortable with the new world society than their parents, which resulted in some loss of parental authority. Because of this, colonies began to devise laws that imposed child obedience requirements, forcing parents to attend to the behavior and education of their children (Bailyn, 1960). This was the first state (colony) foray into education.

Around this time, colonists who were Oxford and Cambridge graduates wanted to begin similar institutions in the colonies. In 1636, the Massachusetts Bay Colony founded Harvard College with an appropriation of 400 pounds (Whitehead, 1973). While the emphasis was on the perpetuation of cultural knowledge, such an institution also served a practical aim to educate clergy and public leaders. By the American Revolution, the colonies had established nine colleges (Rudolph, 1962).

While the English universities were certainly influential in the colonists' development of American universities, they looked to other countries as well. Creation of external boards of control for the new colleges came from Scottish universities and was adopted to place some accountability on the new institutions. Further, the presidents of the new world universities were granted executive authority, unlike the chancellors of English colleges (Thelin, 2004). American colonists seized the opportunity to create new organizational forms based on the perceived best features of other systems. "One could argue that the creation and refinement of this structure—the external board combined with a strong college president—is a legacy of the colonial colleges that has defined and shaped higher education in the United States to this day" (Thelin, 2004, p. 12).

Schools proliferated over the next century, mainly due to increasing immigration from Europe and growth of religious denominations. Each religion or nationality wanted to be responsible for inculcating their particular values to their children, so they developed their own grammar schools (Bailyn, 1960; Butts, 1978). Attendance at school was voluntary, and any attempt to exert state influence or control over education was usually met with fierce resistance from church and local leaders (Bailyn, 1960). This, coupled with westward expansion and greater physical separation between homesteads, led to a decentralized structure of education governance that persists today (Butts, 1978).

Schools were first supported by individual contributions, which started a tradition of external (non-teacher/student) control of education. "Dependent for support upon annual or even less regular gifts, education at all levels during the early formative years came within the direct control, not of those responsible for instruction, but of those who had created and maintained the institutions. When in the eighteenth century a measure of economic maturity made it possible to revert to other, older forms, the tradition of external control was well established" (Bailyn, 1960, p. 44). External control of schools continued even after the American Revolution, when some of the founding fathers desired a national system of education to inculcate republican values (Tyack, James, & Benavot, 1987). "Education—civic as well as intellectual—seemed an ideal instrument to turn people with diverse loyalties into citizens of a new entity—the republican state—while at the same time training them to be alert to their rights, liberties, and responsibilities" (Tyack et al., 1987, p. 24). Yet, a national system of education never took hold, as a coordinated federal effort could not be assembled. There was no mention of education in the Articles of Confederation of 1781 or the U.S. Constitution of 1789. However, the congressional Land Ordinance of 1785 required that new townships include a portion of land for public schools (Bailyn, 1960). This was more to incentivize westward expansion than to support public schooling (Tyack et al., 1987). Lack of federal involvement did not mean that education was absent from governmental agendas; many state constitutions adopted since the revolution had already addressed education (Butts, 1978). For instance, as early as 1784, the state of New York developed a board of regents to oversee and provide financial support for education (Kaestle, 1983). By the late 1800s, all states had some constitutional or statutory provision for education (Tyack et al., 1987).

The 19th century would bring dramatic fluctuations in state support and governance of higher education, which would further its distinction from primary/secondary education. First, higher education shifted from complete state support to more private support. All colonial colleges were legally established by a civil authority (an American colony or British monarchy) and were initially supported and governed by such civil authority. However, by the late 1800s, a distinction between public and private colleges became apparent. First, states began to limit their financial support to the nation's colleges. This was likely due to the rise of state support for common schools (primary grades) and other social welfare activities in the mid-1800s that placed additional demands on state budgets (Whitehead, 1973). This additional state support for common schools stemmed, in part, from court cases resulting in state compulsory attendance laws, requiring students to attend school until a certain age or grade. By 1900, most states had such a law (Hutt, 2012).

Second, Whitehead argues that not only did the rise of common schools require additional funds, but unlike higher education, common schools also had state-supported personnel (superintendents) to lobby legislators and engender support. This was at a time when colleges lacked vast popular support. "The doubts of the people rested on three major contentions—that the colleges were aristocratic, that they were sectarian, and that they were only for the 'professional classes'" (Whitehead, 1973, p. 123). This view did not engender much widespread public demand for greater governmental support of colleges. Further, new territories were required to include provision of education in their constitutions in order to be admitted to statehood (Tyack et al., 1987). The language of most constitutions was stronger for primary and secondary education than higher education (if higher education was mentioned at all). K–12 education was often deemed a right for citizens, but states only had to make provisions for higher education. All of these factors helped to shift a greater proportion of state resources to K–12 education over higher education.

In the mid-1800s, French aristocrat Alexis de Tocqueville (1835), interested in the American democracy "experiment," came to study its government.

He subsequently published his observations. He found that the average educational level of American citizens was greater than in Europe, but yet there were not many "learned" citizens. On the other hand, there were not many "ignorant" people. Tocqueville notes, "in New England, every citizen receives the elementary notions of human knowledge; he is moreover taught the doctrines and the evidences of his religion, the history of his country, and the leading features of its Constitution." (p. 366). He also found that education was not as robust in the western and southern regions of the U.S. during that time. Perhaps what Tocqueville noticed was the effect of valuing education for practical purposes. All people had some education, yet very few were well educated. Knowledge for knowledge's sake was not the core value. Tocqueville compared the aims of education between the U.S. and Europe and found that "in the United States politics are the end and aim of education; in Europe its principal object is to fit men for private life" (p. 370).

Nevertheless, higher education continued to grow during this time period. In 1862, the federal Morrill Act established land-grant colleges in each state for practical mechanical and agricultural education. Institutions specifically for women and Blacks also dotted the landscape. Normal schools for educating teachers numbered in the hundreds, and research became important as the first Ph.D. was offered at Johns Hopkins University in 1876 (Rudolph, 1962). All of these developments increased both the number and the size of higher education institutions.

By 1900, common schools had greatly expanded with the aid of state support and mandatory attendance laws. State-appointed officials governed elementary and secondary education. Higher education had also expanded with a mixture of state and private support, but control rested at the institutional rather than state level. By the turn of the 20th century, it was clear that K–12 and higher education had evolved into separate systems.

Linking the Sectors

With greater numbers of children attending primary and secondary education and more students attending college, the need for greater linkages between the sectors became important.

19th Century History

Following the lead of the University of Michigan in 1871, faculty from various institutions of higher education began visiting feeder high schools to observe the academic program and decide whether graduates of the schools were prepared for college (VanOverbeke, 2008). Graduates of accredited high schools had guaranteed admission to the specific accrediting institution without the need for an entrance exam. This process also benefited the institutions because feeder high schools adopted the curriculum recommended by the university and could ensure graduates would be ready for college courses (VanOverbeke, 2008). There was a larger aim as well. James Angell, the president of the University of Michigan at the time accreditation began, hoped that alignment of expectations throughout the educational levels would lead all teachers and professors to see themselves as "'parts of one united system' working to provide a strong education for all students in the state" (VanOverbeke, 2008, p. 39). Over time, accreditation of feeder high schools by individual colleges and their professors became unwieldy given the growth in the number of high schools students matriculated from, and organizations were established to take over the functions on behalf of regions of institutions.

Early 20th Century History

In the early 1900s, the College Entrance Examination Board (now College Board) developed a uniform assessment for college entry (Karabel, 2005). This helped to establish uniform requirements for college entry and provide common guidance for high school curriculums across the nation. As individual colleges began replacing their assessments with this common examination, a more diverse student body from around the nation had the opportunity to take an entrance exam and be admitted to an institution (Karabel, 2005). This, along with accreditation, began sending signals to K–12, as a sector, on what was required for college entry. Yet, it was generally up to individual schools and districts whether to heed the signals, which resulted in uneven student preparation and access to higher education.

In the early 20th century, the governance divide between K–12 and post-secondary education was marked. Basic education was compulsory and supported by both local and state funding. Local school boards governed the schools under general guidance and requirements from the state. Institutions of higher education received state and federal, rather than local, funding and remained largely independent of state control (Tyack et al., 1987). In fact, in 1940, 70% of postsecondary institutions had their own governing bodies (Kirst, 2005). This changed drastically just a few years later.

The federal Serviceman's Readjustment Act of 1946 (GI Bill) effectively opened higher education to the masses, as returning World War II soldiers entered colleges by the tens of thousands (Kirst, 2005; Thelin, 2004). Coordination was required to accommodate this growth. The decision of how to coordinate higher education at the state level resulted in another major governance disjuncture with secondary education. Rather than place responsibility for higher education coordination under existing state departments of education, new state-level bodies dedicated to higher education were created. This occurred for several reasons. First, it was thought that state departments of education did not have the capacity to handle new responsibilities concerning higher education (Hill & Rabineau, 1969). The departments' existing duties related to higher education primarily focused on data collection and teacher preparation, and even these minor duties were often neglected in favor of focus on K–12 education (Hill & Rabineau, 1969). Even if the departments had the capacity to accommodate higher education, there were other reasons why higher education institutions did not want to be under the auspices of the state departments of education. Hill and Rabineau (1969) claim that many higher education administrators saw department personnel as bureaucrats beholden to politicians, depending on whether the chief state school officer and/or state board of education was elected. Further, some higher education leaders feared that association with a politically elected governing authority would hamper academic freedom. Many affiliated with higher education observed the centralization of K–12 education under state departments of education and did not want to fall into that same model. The lobby was successful, and most states developed separate bodies to coordinate and/or govern institutions of higher education (Hill & Rabineau, 1969).

Late 20th Century History

Two-year community colleges and technical colleges require special mention regarding linkages with K–12 education. Many colleges were funded through local property taxes, much like K–12 schools, and the nomenclature of professionals mirrored K–12 education more than higher education (e.g., community college teachers were called instructors rather than professors) (Kirst, 2005; Thelin, 2004). Starting in the 1970s, as community colleges' missions expanded, along with their student bodies, to include vocational education and community service, they began to move to their own statewide governance structures—either with existing higher education agencies or as separate systems (Kirst, 2005). A noticeable increase in students needing remediation upon entering these colleges was evident after the break with state and local departments of education (Kirst, 2005). Burton Clark (1985) notes that higher education's failure to downward-couple with secondary education is somewhat unique to the United States. Other countries have tighter governance linkages between the two sectors, which ostensibly help to create a more seamless education pipeline (Timpane, 1999).

The Current Structure of American Education

As noted previously, the U.S. Constitution does not contain provisions for any level of education. Therefore, it remains the province of states. The brief history in this chapter details how education developed in the states, which leads us to where we are now. Subsequent chapters detail the specific authority of local, state, and federal governments over different sectors of education. In many instances authority is shared, and in some cases authority is not granted per rule or law but obtained through provision of funding.

Some have called this complicated structure a "tangled web" (Epstein, 2006), while others may note that the American education system simply reflects its federalist heritage. Whatever one may call it, it remains that the American system is unique in its fragmentation, as several other developed countries maintain a more cohesive system. In fact, the countries that outperform the United States on international student benchmarking exams, such as Australia, Finland, and Singapore, have centralized education structures where ultimate authority and accountability for education are well-defined (Tucker, 2013).

In contrast, there are several places where the American education "buck stops."[1] Partly, accountability depends on the level of education—early childhood, K–12, or post-secondary. It also depends on whether one is considering public education or the entire system of public and private institutions. Within each level of education, there are multiple accountability points. For instance, federal and state governments play important roles in early childhood education, as do private providers. In K–12 education, local and state boards of education hold legal responsibility for outcomes, but an argument could be made that the federal government has some accountability given its involvement through funding and programs. For both early childhood and K–12 education, perhaps the family and student bear some accountability as well. In higher education, the onus of accountability has traditionally settled upon the student, but now that appears to be shifting more to the institution and state with a dose of responsibility for the federal government, given the vast amount of funding provided to students and institutions.

To make this more concrete, imagine that a parent of a fifth grade public school student takes issue with newly adopted science learning standards. To whom does that parent complain? The teacher who might rightfully claim that he is only teaching the standards given to him by his principal? The principal who might rightfully claim that she is only passing the standards down from the school district superintendent? The superintendent who might rightfully claim that he is only implementing the standards as adopted by the local school board? The local school board that might rightfully claim they are only adopting standards approved by the state board of education? The state board of education that might rightfully claim they only adopted new standards due to pressure from the state's governor? A state's governor who might rightfully claim that she is only encouraging the appointed state board to adopt federally sanctioned standards to ensure continued receipt of federal funding? The president of the United States who might rightfully say that the federal government has no official role regarding education and all decisions are made by the state? There may be very sound policy reasons for adopting new learning standards—including increasing rigor and updating knowledge—but what entity or office ultimately takes accountability for this and other decisions remains fluid.

Role of Law/Courts

There are several avenues of redress should a person or group want to see changes in education policies. The executive branch can enforce existing laws and rules; the legislative branch can create, amend, or rescind laws; and the judicial branch can intervene if laws are not applied properly or are unconstitutional (Dayton, 2012). All three branches of federal and state governments—executive, legislative, judicial—have an impact on policies because the branches are designed to provide checks and balances upon each other. However, the courts' role in shaping public policies, including education, is often overlooked and misunderstood.

Part of the consternation over the courts' role in policy comes from a lack of clarity about what they do and how they work. Legal and other scholars disagree about whether courts should merely adjudicate disputes through application of prior law (precedent) or interpret sources of law through current contextual lenses. Either way, there is bound to be some impact on education policy. For example, application of prior law to a new dispute still requires a court to determine that the new dispute falls in the same category as the dispute that created the prior law. In *New Jersey v. T.L.O.* (1985), the court found that public school administrators did not need "probable cause" to search students but merely "reasonable suspicion," given the need to maintain a safe learning environment. Later, a lower court applied the *T.L.O.* precedent to *Burnham v. West* (1987) in deciding that the smell of marijuana outside of a school cafeteria did not provide reasonable suspicion to search students' backpacks and purses (Bosher, Kaminski, & Vacca, 2004). Certainly, interpreting sources of law through current contextual lenses creates new policy, as seen with segregation of public schools. In 1896, the U.S. Supreme Court decided that separate but equal schools for Black and White students was constitutional (*Plessy v. Ferguson*, 1896). In 1954, the U.S. Supreme Court decided that separate but equal schools were unconstitutional and ordered integration (*Brown v. Board of Education*, 1954). Sometimes legal opinions are not as clear as rendering a policy unconstitutional or not. The Supreme Court's decisions over the past 30 years on the consideration of race in higher education admissions have consistently added nuance after nuance so that lawyers are (or should be) involved in setting colleges' admission policies.

The judicial system, like most government systems, is very complex. There are courts at the local, state, and federal levels. Courts at each of those levels have certain subject-matter jurisdiction. Notably, the U.S. Constitution's 10th Amendment reserves educational issues to the states, but federal courts may address education through other constitutional provisions such as the 14th Amendment, which is frequently used to protect civil rights, or the 4th Amendment, which covers search and seizure law. Complexity also begets a slow process. Courts must decide whether a person has standing to bring a case to court—as not every grievance merits review—and whether the proper parties bring the dispute to the proper type of court. If the court takes up the case, the process of evidence gathering and adjudication can be very lengthy. Sometimes, as was the case with public school racial integration, there may be several cases before impactful precedent is set because each case focuses on a narrow set of legal concepts. The slow process is not necessarily a bad thing, as it can "limit the risks of reactionary, rash decisions or the dangers of mob rule" (Dayton, 2012, p. 19). On the other hand, not all meritorious cases make it before a court because "limited agenda space can make it hard for issues to break through" (Henig, 2013, p. 83).

Much attention is placed on U.S. Supreme Court education cases because those opinions apply to educational institutions in all 50 states. Generally, the court has declined an active education policymaking role. A notable exception may be the period of time between 1950 and the turn of the 21st century. Prior to 1950, education was seen as a local issue, and lower courts usually only interfered in student injury cases or contract disputes (McCarthy, 2008). A general expansion of judicial policymaking occurred in the mid-20th century. Educational issues were included in this expansion as the court "extended constitutional protection to vulnerable groups" (McCarthy, 2008, p. 112). This, of course, included *Brown*, but it also included cases stemming from Congress's passage of the Civil Rights Act of 1964. For example, the court in *Lau v. Nichols* (1974) held that schools violated Title VI of the Civil Rights Act by not providing Chinese-speaking students special assistance with the English language.

From 2009 to 2014, the court did not rule on any K–12 public school cases (Walsh, 2014). There are several possible reasons for this, including the court's historical reluctance to substitute their judgment for that of educational policymakers and leaders; the significantly decreased volume of cases the court now decides each term; and the movement of education reform issues to nonjudicial avenues (Walsh, 2014). Several education-related court cases (at all court levels) in the 19th century considered the proper scope of the public school system. Should it include kindergarten, high school, and/or normal schools for teachers (early training schools)? Should schools teach Latin? Should taxes be used to outfit schoolrooms with such extravagances as maps and globes? Although the specifics have changed, these types of questions are still being asked (e.g. "should charter schools be allowed?" and "should community colleges be free to students?"), but now they are usually debated by the executive and legislative branches of government rather than the courts.

Who Makes Education Policy

At any level of government that has some jurisdiction over education, there are several types of people involved in educational policymaking. Most visible are elected general government leaders: the president, governors, and in some cases, mayors. Most of these elected leaders utilize at least part of their bully pulpit and political influence on educational issues.

Given that the federal government has no legal jurisdiction over education, U.S. presidents are limited in their policymaking role. Every president has displayed varying levels of interest and activity in education policy. Presidents can affect education policy in two main ways: budget power and appointment power. By funding existing and new programs and shaping the regulations around those programs, the president can have a fair amount of influence on education policy. For example, President George W. Bush's revamp of the 1965 Elementary and Secondary Education Act, passed by Congress in 2001 as the No Child Left Behind Act, affected each state's education accountability system. Because states accepted NCLB funding from the federal government, they were beholden to the associated rules. The rules included creating new data systems to collect and monitor student progress, increasing qualifications for teachers, offering school choice options, and sanctioning nonperforming schools. This produced quite an effect on education policy trickling down from the federal government to states to classrooms.

Presidents also have appointment powers. The most visible and probably most important appointment is the U.S. Secretary of Education who administers hundreds of millions of dollars and hires thousands of staff. There are also boards such as the National Assessment Governing Board, which administers the National Assessment of Educational Progress (a national student academic benchmarking exam), as well as various ad-hoc committees, such as those used by President Lyndon Johnson in designing the original Head Start and Elementary and Secondary Education Acts.

State governors are taking greater roles in educational policymaking because education is increasingly tied to state economic development goals. Although governors have varying levels of influence and power across states, they do have a common set of tools that they can use to influence the shape of education. These include the ability to: develop agendas that identify policy priorities and to use their bully pulpits to garner public and legislative support for them; foster relationships with legislators, especially if the governor is also the head of his/her state political party; develop and submit a budget to the legislature that often becomes the foundation for budget negotiations; exercise control over executive branch agencies and their resources; and appoint education boards and trustees.

Both presidents and governors have some power to enact policies through executive orders and regulations, but Congress and state legislatures have the primary tool to create policies: the ability to introduce legislation that can become law. As noted previously, President George W. Bush is credited with developing the No Child Left Behind Act, but Senator Edward Kennedy and several members of the House of Representatives certainly had a large role in writing and shaping the legislation along with securing passage in Congress. Further, at both national and state levels, legislators consider how a policy (in the form of legislation) will affect their local constituencies. Although legislators are acting on national or state policies, they still represent the citizens of a certain geographical area.

Mayors, especially those of large urban cities, may have some influence on education policy. First, they can use notoriety to publicize educational issues in the city. Second, they may use their influence to convene different education stakeholders to address certain education policies. Third, some mayors are gaining concrete authority over K–12 education as the plight of urban education worsens and citizens look for change. This has occurred in urban metropolitan areas such as Washington, DC, New York City, and Boston. Finally, mayors and city councils may have some authority over the distribution of local funds for educational purposes.

Also at the local level, elected local boards of K–12 education adopt policies that affect local schools and classrooms. For instance, if a state adopts new learning standards and assessments, the local board of education will adopt policies for curriculum materials acquisition and set the qualifications to hire teachers who can successfully implement those standards. Local boards of education also often determine local salary schedules, negotiate with local unions, and determine allocation of funding to individual schools.

Beyond the elected officials described above, there are several appointed bodies that affect education policy. At the state level, boards of education, regents, and commissions adopt regulations to implement legislation and other programs. For example, if a state legislature passes a broad law requiring college presidents to be assessed on institutional completion rates, the state board of regents will have several important decisions to make, including: How will completion rates be calculated? Will rates only include first-time, full-time freshman, or will transfer students be included? What will the target completion rate be for each president? Will it be based on improvement or just a target number? Will completion rates be the only criterion on which these presidents are judged? The answers to these questions would certainly affect policy at the state and institutional levels.

Many of these boards also undergo strategic planning processes to develop visions for their respective areas. Governors, legislators, and other stakeholders are sometimes part of this process. Boards typically meet once per month or less and are composed of volunteers with "day jobs"; therefore, they must have a limited agenda. Limited time and a vast amount of responsibility require boards at every level to prioritize. What a board chooses to focus on has implications for educational policies.

An agency executive implements most board policies. For example, state boards of education usually work in concert with a chief state school officer, and higher education commissions or regents work with a chancellor. Often, the respective boards appoint these agency leaders in consultation with the governor and/or legislative leaders, as it is important for the agency leader to be able to work effectively with all state policy leaders. State education agency leaders often design the organizational structure of the agency, manage the budget, hire personnel, and communicate policy priorities to the public. These duties, among others, can have quite a big impact on educational policies. For example, how the chief state school officer organizes the department of education communicates the relative priority of different educational policies and programs. Consider the attention and visibility a charter schools program would receive if it were a division reporting directly to the state superintendent rather than an office buried four levels down in the bureaucracy. Agency leaders are also often given the opportunity to make speeches or presentations to community groups, media, and the public. A state chancellor of higher education has to determine what policy priorities to emphasize in those talks. Does he or she want to send a public message to the legislature on the need for more student financial assistance, or to the state superintendent of education for better-prepared high school graduates, or to the public about the overall importance of higher education and the efficient use of tax dollars on the enterprise? These examples are just a few ways that agency leaders can influence education policy.

Researcher Lyman Glenny introduced a new type of educational policymaker—the anonymous kind. Although his 1972 article focused on higher education policymaking, it is very relevant to all levels of education. Glenny (1972) argued that as institutional (system, district, state, federal) responsibilities grow, policymakers increasingly rely on professional staff—the anonymous leaders—to gather, interpret, and communicate data and research to them. Through these duties, professional staff can have a large impact on educational policy. Sometimes referred to as bureaucrats, these professionals are often in the agency or system longer than the elected officials or appointed leaders, and that longevity usually brings a wealth of expertise and significant relationships with others involved in policy work (Kingdon, 2011). In his article, Glenny (1972) mainly focuses on institutional staff while briefly highlighting the role of state agency staff and gubernatorial budget staff in education policy decision making. However, 40 years later, I argue that agency and gubernatorial staff roles have greatly expanded beyond what Glenny witnessed in 1972.

To illustrate the point, I want to focus on governors' education policy advisors (GEPAs)—a role that does not get a lot of research or popular attention but has a significant influence on state education policy.[2] The exact function and stature of a GEPA varies by state and governor, but there are some common features of the position. GEPAs are often asked to help craft and implement the governor's agenda, liaison between the governor's office and education stakeholders, and manage the flow of information to the governor. These are certainly influential functions, and it is possible the GEPA role sometimes comes at the expense of using agency leaders as advisors to the governor. A 1986 survey of governors found that they relied on education policy advisors more than agency heads or university presidents for higher education policy counsel (Hines, 1988). Rosenthal (2013) cites another survey in which only one in five governors reported extensive involvement by departments and agencies in crafting the gubernatorial agenda. Perhaps GEPAs are more of the policy "wonks" while agency leaders are professional managers. Managing state agencies is not a small job when millions or billions of dollars need to be administered and hundreds or thousands of staff need to be supervised.

Another aspect of the GEPA's role is gatekeeping—controlling the flow of information to the governor. This role is becoming more and more of a necessity as the amount of information (data, reports, briefings) grows exponentially and more and more stakeholders wish to have access to the governor. This intersects with the agency liaison role, because GEPAs must often negotiate agreements between agencies, especially if there are multiple agencies with jurisdiction over a particular topic. For example, Georgia has separate agencies for the university system and for student finance. Both have interest in policies concerning the state's merit aid program, and the governor's advisor plays a key role in negotiating any differences between the agencies before key policy questions are brought to the governor's attention.

Beyond the official roles described previously, there are other entities and forces that influence education policy, such as interest groups and public opinion. Their influence will be touched on throughout this book as they relate to each sector of education, but it is important to mention their unique influence in education policy. Education policy, unlike some other policies, affects a critical mass of people, and the policies can have enormous influence. Education is often the largest expenditure in a state budget; school districts are often the largest employer in an area; thriving businesses require a qualified workforce; and most adults are products of the public education system. There are a lot of interests and a lot of opinions. Education-related interest groups and popular opinion on educational issues are difficult for elected officials to ignore.

Conclusion

The American education structure is made of many moving parts. It is certainly complex, if not entirely coherent and coordinated. As the following chapters will help illustrate, simple solutions for any types of "improvements" are difficult to come by. This is not necessarily because the policy leaders or staff or teachers are incompetent, but rather, the structure itself may pose obstacles. There are inherent, long-standing tensions stemming from how the overall system was historically shaped that work to prevent the seamless flow of students from high school to college or from technical/community colleges to four-year colleges; the traditional structure was not designed to accommodate the wide pipeline needed to meet today's educational goals. Structural tensions also exist between who controls education. In the beginning, there was a strong emphasis on local community control of schools. That is changing somewhat as states and the nation are trying to compete in a global economy. Governors are courting foreign companies to do business in their respective states, and they must present a qualified and ready workforce. They want (and perhaps need) more control to ensure optimal educational outcomes.

The values that Americans hold dear also create tensions that make education reform difficult. In *Brown v. Board of Education* (1954), Americans stood for individual equality of opportunity for all students to succeed. This was reinforced through the 2001 No Child Left Behind legislation. This noble value often conflicts with another great American value—that of the market system. A capitalistic economy rewards extra effort and places a premium on knowledge. So, while we want everyone to have a chance, we know that some will "win" and others will "lose."[3] These tensions do not mean that American education is doomed to a downward spiral; rather, they mean that we must first define what we mean by "improvement" and then not settle for simplistic solutions that do not take into account the complicated nature of the education system.

For Further Information

- The Center on Education Governance at the University of Southern California provides information on several areas concerning the structure of education: www.uscrossier.org/ceg/
- The Program on Education Policy and Governance in Harvard University's government department covers K–12 governance issues: www.hks.harvard.edu/pepg/
- This U.S. Department of Education website provides information on the structure of American Education: www2.ed.gov/about/offices/list/ous/international/usnei/us/edlite-structure-us.html
- David O'Brien's book *Storm Center: The Supreme Court in American Politics* (9th ed.) is a very readable account of U.S. Supreme Court operations that illuminates the court's role in public policy issues.

Notes

1. A phrase that Marc Tucker uses in his 2013 report to discuss placement of ultimate accountability in international education governance structures.
2. Much of the discussion here also pertains to education policy advisors at the federal level (to the president of the United States and the secretary of education), congressional committee staff, and to professionalized state legislative staff.
3. For an in-depth discussion of the structural and value-laden tensions in American education, see David Labaree's *Someone Has to Fail* (2010).

References

Bailyn, B. (1960). *Education in the forming of American society.* Chapel Hill: University of North Carolina at Chapel Hill.

Bosher, W., Jr., Kaminski, K., & Vacca, R. (2004). *The school law handbook: What every leader needs to know.* Alexandria, VA: Association for Supervision and Curriculum Development.

Brown v. Board of Education of Topeka, 347 U.S. 483 (1954).

Burnham v. West, 681 F. Supp. 1160 (E.D. Va. 1987).

Butts, R. (1978). *Public education in the United States: From revolution to reform*. New York, NY: Holt, Rinehart, & Winston.

Clark, B. (Ed.). (1985). *The school and the university: An international perspective*. Berkeley: University of California Press.

Dayton, J. (2012). *Education law: Principles, policies, and practice*. Wisdom Builders Press: Bangor, ME.

Epstein, N. (2006). *Who's in charge here? The tangled web of school governance and policy*. Washington, DC: Brookings Institution Press.

Glenny, L. (1972). The anonymous leaders of higher education. *The Journal of Higher Education, 43*(1), 9–22.

Henig, J. (2013). *The end of exceptionalism in American education*. Cambridge, MA: Harvard Education Press.

Hill, W., & Rabineau, L. (1969). Higher education relationships. In W. Hill & L. Rabineau (Eds.), *Education in the states: Nationwide development since 1900*. Washington, DC: National Education Association.

Hines, E. (1988). *Higher education and state governments: Renewed partnership, cooperation, or competition?* (Report No. 5). Washington, DC: Association for the Study of Higher Education.

Hutt, E. (2012). Formalism over function: Compulsion, courts, and the rise of educational formalism in America, 1870–1930. *Teachers College Record, 114*, 1–27.

Kaestle, C. (1983). *Pillars of the republic: Common schools and American society, 1780–1860*. New York, NY: Hill and Wang.

Karabel, J. (2005). *The chosen*. New York, NY: Mariner Books.

Kingdon, J. (2011). *Agendas, Alternatives, and Public Policies* 2nd ed. Boston, MA: Longman.

Kirst, M. (2005, June 1). *Separation of K–12 and postsecondary education governance and policymaking: Evolution and impact*. Retrieved from www.stanford.edu/group/bridgeproject/Separation%20of%20K-12%20and%20Postsec%20Ed%20Governance%20and%20Policymak.pdf

Labaree, D. (2010). *Someone has to fail*. Cambridge, MA: Harvard University Press.

Lau v. Nichols, 414 U.S. 563 (1974).

McCarthy, M. (2008). Judicial Impact on Education Politics and Policies. In Handbook of Education Politics and Policy (Cooper, B., Cibulka, J., & Fusarelli, L, Eds.). New York: Routledge. 109–125.

McGuinn, P., & Manna, P. (2013). Education governance in America: Who leads when everyone is in charge? In P. Manna & P. McGuinn (Eds.), *Education governance for the twenty-first century: Overcoming the structural barriers to school reform*.

Washington, DC: Thomas B. Fordham Institute, Center for American Progress, Brookings Institution Press.

New Jersey v. T.L.O., 469 U.S. 325 (1985).

Plessy v. Ferguson, 163 U.S. 537 (1896).

Rosenthal, A. (2013). *The best job in politics: Exploring how governors succeed as policy leaders.* Los Angeles, CA: Sage Press.

Rudolph, F. (1962). *The American college & university.* Athens: University of Georgia Press.

Thelin, J. (2004). *A history of American higher education.* Baltimore, MA: Johns Hopkins University Press.

Timpane, M. (1999). *Higher education and the schools.* Washington, DC: Institute for Educational Leadership.

Tocqueville, A. de (1835). *Democracy in America.* New York, NY: Bantam Books.

Tucker, M. (2013). *Governing American education: Why this dry subject may hold the key to advances in American education.* Retrieved from www.ncee.org/wp-content/uploads/2013/10/Governing-American-Education.pdf

Tyack, D., James, T., & Benavot, A. (1987). *Law and the shaping of public education 1785–1954.* Madison: The University of Wisconsin Press.

VanOverbeke, M. (2008). *The standardization of American schooling: Linking secondary and higher education, 1870–1910.* New York, NY: Palgrave.

Walsh, M. "After Decades of Action, Supreme Court Cools on School Cases," *Education Week,* October 1, 2014.

Whitehead, J. (1973). *The separation of college and state.* New Haven, CT: Yale University Press.

Chapter 3

Theories of the Policy Process[1]

Introduction

For those involved in education, it may sometimes seem that the system operates and changes in a random and/or confusing fashion. Policies seem to appear out of nowhere and then may disappear over time or perhaps more abruptly when a new official such as a governor, state superintendent, or chancellor is installed in office. Further, the education policy process is very complex because it involves many stakeholders (e.g., elected officials, interest groups, and teachers), happens over a long period of time, engages several levels of government, and usually concerns deeply held values and/or priorities. "In short, understanding the policy process requires knowledge of the goals and perceptions of hundreds of actors throughout the country involving possibly very technical scientific and legal issues over periods of a decade or more while most of those actors are actively seeking to propagate their specific 'spin' on events" (Sabatier, 2007, p. 4). Researchers have long attempted to make sense of the public policymaking process by examining such things as how policies get placed on an official's agenda, how they develop, and how they spread across communities and states. To make sense of these phenomena, scholars have developed a number of conceptual frameworks, theories, and models. Sometimes, such as with conceptual frameworks, researchers identify the elements or variables of a context and the relationship between them. Theories tend to be more specific in hypothesizing the direction of relationships (e.g., this causes that). Often, these theories help make sense of how education policies go from idea to classroom. This chapter will provide a brief introduction to some of the more relevant policy theories to education in order to provide readers with additional context with which to think critically about education policy.

It is important to understand up front that while theories provide some context for the education policy landscape, the policymaking process is still messy. For example, researcher Lorraine McDonnell explains:

> Policy making is rarely linear—moving from problem definition to design, agenda setting, enactment, and finally implementation. Rather, policy options may exist before a problem is defined, and during implementation, policies may cycle back for new enactments or fall off the agenda altogether.
>
> (McDonnell & Weatherford, 2013, p. 4)

Many of us may initially believe we understand how policy works without the need for theories. However, theories help analysts, researchers, and educators view policy processes through a more organized lens. Our own unstructured analysis may be complicated with "internal inconsistencies, ambiguities, erroneous assumptions, and invalid propositions" because there is nothing to test it against (Sabatier, 2007, p. 5). Theories provide a frame for applying our knowledge and insights by identifying variables to which we should be paying attention and helping to organize what we observe (Sabatier, 2007); therefore, they may provide a more unbiased filter than our own common sense.

A very simple and rational conception of the policy process separates the process into stages: agenda setting, policy definition, implementation, evaluation, and decision making about the future of the policy/program (Ripley, 2010). Agenda setting concerns what policy issues rise to the attention of policymakers. Given the infinite number of policy issues that could be addressed and the limited capacity of time and resources, policymakers must prioritize what they focus on. Agenda setting includes identifying which policy issues are "problems" and must be addressed (Ripley, 2010). The policy definition stage includes identifying and analyzing various potential solutions to the identified policy problem. This usually involves various interest groups and stakeholders weighing in on the options/solutions with negotiations taking place between various policy actors. The end result of this stage could be legislation, an executive order, or other policy pronouncement. The next phase of a basic policy process, program implementation, involves further defining and planning for the new policy, program, or initiative created to solve the problem or issue. This is usually done at a staff, rather than policymaker, level. Sometimes, in the case of major policy change, agency boards must adopt regulations that further define the new policy. For example, if a state legislature identifies a problem of inadequate kindergarten readiness and passes a law creating a public pre-kindergarten program, the state agency overseeing early childhood efforts will plan for and possibly implement regulations for the new program. Finally, the policy process includes evaluation of the new policy. Questions could include whether the policy had the intended short- and long-term impacts, whether there were any unintended impacts, and whether any changes are needed to the policy. This informs future decision making about the policy.

While this is very helpful in conceptualizing the perhaps ideal process, it is important to again remember that policymaking hardly ever happens in such a linear fashion, given starts and stops, looking for solutions to problems, unexpected pockets of funding to be spent, and pet projects that can derail any kind of rational policy process. The conceptualized stages of policymaking don't necessarily occur chronologically or separately.

So, just as we all might hope that we behave in a rational fashion most of the time, we also hope our policies are made in the manner depicted previously. While there are several policy process theories that offer a more nuanced and realistic view than the rational model, the following five policy theories tend to be frequently utilized in education policy analyses.

Incrementalism

First, most similar to rationality is incrementalism. A theory of incrementalism suggests that policy builds gradually over time. "Instead of beginning consideration of each program or issue afresh, decision makers take what they are currently doing as given, and make small, incremental, marginal adjustments in that current behavior" (Kingdon, 2011, p. 79). The theory is used most often when examining development of policy proposals and policy alternatives rather than how an item gets placed on policymakers' agendas (Kingdon, 2011).

The best example of incrementalism can be found in educational budgets. Budgets are often deemed an entity's primary policy mechanism because how a school district or college or state allocates its funding indicates its priorities. For example, state policymakers can decide to allocate new funds to begin or expand a pre-kindergarten program, provide for teacher raises, or provide school districts money for new buses, among several other options. The decisions policymakers make about budgets signal priorities.

Under the theory of incremental budgeting, there are three primary actions a governmental body can take using the prior year's budget as a baseline: They can award new allocations, recommend reallocations, or call for deductions. New allocations stem from a new (e.g., implementation of a lottery program) or expanded (e.g., greater tax receipts) revenue source. Funds can also be reallocated. If one policy is not working or is no longer in favor, funds can be transferred to a new or existing policy. Interestingly, state agency leaders must often be careful of what they request in upcoming budgets; sometimes governors and legislatures merely say "yes" to the new program or policy without providing additional funding, and they expect the agency to internally reallocate funding to incorporate the new program into its work. Finally, governments can deduct funding from budgets. This can happen through across-the-board cuts, often in times of economic recession, or through targeted cuts. Again, cutting a program from the budget signals a large policy shift. For example, many states that used to provide salary stipends to teachers for earning National Board Teacher Certification eliminated or significantly reduced those line items in their budgets, resulting in a drastic reduction in the number of teachers who sought such certification.

While incrementalism may simply seem like the path of least resistance for policymakers, imagine hitting delete on the spreadsheets that depict the current budget and starting with just one large number on the screen—the amount of revenue generated by the state, district, agency, or college. With only this one number to work from, those preparing the budget and policymakers must think through and justify each expenditure. While that might be a good idea every so often, it would effectively cripple a governmental entity if done each year given the time and resources needed to do this.

Beyond budgets, one could potentially apply the theory of incrementalism to the creation of the nation's entire system of mandatory public education. The system initially started with grammar school then expanded to high school. Now, most states offer free pre-kindergarten programs, and President Obama just recommended that the first two years of college be free as well. Rather than fundamentally change the educational system to enhance learning and achieve objectives, it may just be easier to incrementally expand the years one attends. Incrementalism is a very common sense, practical theory of policy development, but it does not fully account for the complexity and/or change in education policy. These next theories attempt to do this.

Multiple Streams

Utilizing extensive research on policymaking at the federal level, Kingdon (2011) developed a theory of policymaking that accounts for the ambiguity inherent in many organizations. The theory is often referred to as the *multiple streams framework*, and it is frequently utilized in education policy research. The multiple streams framework builds upon earlier theories that characterized some organizations, particularly education institutions, as organized anarchies (Cohen, March, & Olsen, 1972). Organized anarchies are characterized by inconsistent and ill-defined preferences, unclear technology (all of the organization's processes are not clearly understood by participants), and fluid participation (people in the organization devote attention and effort to different policy items at different times) (Cohen et al., 1972). The complexity of educational organizations and the wide variety of expectations set upon them lend credence to the view of educational organizations as organized anarchies.

Specific to organized anarchies is a "garbage can" theory of decision-making (Cohen et al., 1972). A decision-making opportunity can be viewed as a garbage can "into which various kinds of problems and solutions are dumped by participants as they are generated" (p. 2). Sometimes the problems and solutions come together and a policy decision is made. The authors note:

> It is clear that the garbage can process does not resolve problems well. But it does enable choices to be made and problems resolved, even when the organization is plagued with goal ambiguity and conflict, with poorly understood problems that wander in and out of the system, with a variable environment, and with decision makers who may have other things on their minds.
>
> (Cohen et al., 1972, p. 16)

Kingdon (2011) expanded on and extended this theory by explaining *how* policies come to the forefront of an agenda so that a decision can be made. Each of these theoretical components will be explained in turn.

In essence, the multiple streams framework recognizes that policymaking often does not happen in a linear or incremental fashion. So, in this type of nonrational environment, how are policy agendas—the key policy items policymakers attempt to take action on—developed? Kingdon (2011) suggests that problems, solutions, and politics (the three streams) flow independently in the environment. For example, expert staff in the migrant education office may be working on solutions to improve migrant students' education, but unless that is coupled with a problem (as defined next) related to migrant education and the politics are ripe, solutions to migrant education issues will not make it to the visible policy agenda.

Before an issue becomes a problem requiring a policymaker's attention, Kingdon (2011) calls it a *condition*. Think of weight management. A person could know he/she is overweight (a condition), but it may not become a condition requiring attention until diabetes is contracted or a heart attack occurs. This is a rather unfortunate example, but people are much like organizations with only a finite amount of time and attention to focus on issues. In organizations, conditions can become problems under certain circumstances. Indicators (e.g., kindergarten readiness, high school graduation rates) can elevate a condition to a policymaker's attention if the indicator becomes too small, too large, or changes abruptly. A focusing event, such as a crisis or disaster, could also highlight a condition. Finally, feedback received by the policymaker through formal (e.g., evaluation studies) or informal (e.g., constituent feed-back) mechanisms can move a condition to a possible problem (Kingdon, 2011). An elevated condition becomes a problem requiring focus if the con-dition violates important values, if comparison of the condition with similar conditions signals an issue (e.g., U.S. international ranking on attainment rates falls), or if a condition is reclassified (e.g., situating racial and socioeconomic disparities in educational attainment as an international competitiveness issue). Once a problem is elevated to a policymaker's attention, it does not stay there indefinitely. A problem may fade when it is addressed or the attempt to address it fails, the conditions that brought the problem to light change, more pressing conditions replace it, people forget about it, and/or the public grows used to the condition and does not see it as a problem any longer (Kingdon, 2011).

The politics stream revolves around changes in leadership, interest group activity, and public opinion. Leadership change includes shifts in adminis-trations (e.g., new governors, chancellors) or changes in partisanship such as a transition from Republican- to Democratic-majority legislature. Often new leaders or regimes highlight new conditions and problems rather than continuing work on existing ones. Changes in national mood can also affect the political stream and hence the possibility for policy decisions (Kingdon, 2011). For example, one reason for greater accountability efforts in the K–12 sector than in higher education may be due to greater public dissatisfaction with K–12 (Doyle & Kirst, 2015).

Finally, as noted previously in the migrant education example, the solu-tions stream is ongoing, mainly through the work of bureaucrats or staff-level experts who are constantly examining their particular policy issue and figuring out ways to make it better. Solutions could also appear in white papers issued by think tanks and interest groups. Individual policy entre-preneurs may also have a role in touting certain solutions, as discussed later. How a particular policy proposal (solution) is chosen depends on a num-ber of factors, including technical feasibility, congruence with the values of community members, and anticipation of future constraints such as funding, public acceptability, and politicians' receptivity (Kingdon, 2011).

When the problems, solutions, and politics streams merge around a par-ticular issue, a policy window opens. Sometimes these windows are pre-dictable, such as when legislation is up for renewal. Most other times, the windows are unpredictable and are usually open for a small amount of time (Kingdon, 2011). "Open windows present opportunities for the complete linkage of problems, proposals, and politics, and hence opportunities to move packages of the three joined elements up on decision agenda" (Kingdon, 2011, p. 204).

Policy entrepreneurs have a role in coupling the streams and opening policy windows. An entrepreneur can be anyone involved in the policymaking process who is willing to spend time and resources advocating for a certain policy or policies and has some access to policymakers. Elected officials, high-level bureaucrats, journalists, academics, business people, and community leaders are just some examples of potential policy entrepreneurs. Policy entrepreneurs "use several activities to promote their ideas. These include identifying problems, networking in policy circles, shaping the terms of policy debates, and building coalitions" (Mintrom, 1997, p. 739). It is important for these entrepreneurs to build credibility for the policies for which they are advocating. This can include the use of research. Although entrepreneurs could use research strategically (e.g., only highlighting positive research), their interest in maintaining credibility may mitigate selective presentation of research (McDonnell & Weatherford, 2013). School choice is a recent and popular topic for policy entrepreneurs. A 1997 study found that policy entrepreneurs were critical in getting school choice on state legislative agendas for consideration, but not as successful in getting legislation passed, because strong opposition—in this case, teachers' unions—can thwart policy entrepreneurs' efforts (Mintrom, 1997).

Punctuated Equilibrium

The punctuated equilibrium theory is somewhat similar to the multiple streams framework in that it focuses on how policies appear on highly visible political and policy agendas, but it differs slightly from the multiple streams framework in explaining how it happens. The basis of the theory, adapted from theories of evolution, is that political processes and policy agendas remain largely stable over time with perhaps some incremental policy changes (True, Jones, & Baumgartner, 2007). During these times of equilibrium, policy issues are the domains of technical experts, such as bureaucrats, that consistently focus on the policy. Data are analyzed, tweaks are made, and considerations for substantial improvement may occur, but the policy issues remain off of the visible political and policy agendas. Throughout this period of stability are brief bursts of significant policy change, or *punctuations,* when an issue rises from the policy subsystem (technical experts) to the larger political and policy agenda (True et al., 2007). These punctuations may occur in a surprising fashion or build over time (True et al., 2007). They happen when the policy image (how a policy is currently understood) or issue definition changes or is not agreed upon (True et al., 2007). Political actors are often instrumental in creating or highlighting a policy image change (McLendon & Cohen-Vogel, 2008).

A very recent example that may illustrate this theory of the policy process is occurring in Georgia. For years, Georgia and the majority of other states have been working to improve persistently failing schools. From time to time, federal and state leaders have paid attention to these schools through implementation of more rigorous and detailed accountability systems and new school improvement methods. After Georgia's implementation of new federally mandated accountability systems in the early 2000s, the work of school improvement had largely been left to the technical experts in the state department of education and local school districts. A punctuation occurred in January 2015, when Governor Nathan Deal was reelected and called for the creation of an opportunity school district to takeover persistently failing schools. This call raised school improvement efforts to the macro political state agenda as it called for a constitutional amendment to be voted on by the people of Georgia. The news media, think tanks, advocacy groups, and other politicos are all now weighing in on school improvement issues. It could be that Governor Deal successfully broke through the stasis or equilibrium in this policy realm by changing the policy image from one of incremental improvement of poor performing schools that people would feel relatively satisfied with (things are better than they used to be) to indignant impatience that the lack of significant improvement was hurting students (things are improving too slowly and causing harm).

Evidence supporting punctuated equilibrium theory was found in Mills's (2007) study of change in Florida's higher education governance structure. The citizens of Florida approved a 1998 state constitutional referendum to allow the governor more control over state government through appointing key agency leaders, including the commissioner of education. This caused higher education governance to be a key macro political agenda item from 2000 to 2002, as the state legislature had an opportunity to decide how to implement the successful referendum.

Once a policy has punctuated the equilibrium and is on the larger political agenda, the new policy image becomes a new point of stability and institutional structures change to accommodate the new policy image (Smith & Larimer, 2013). While punctuated equilibrium helps describe policy change, it does not predict it. Still, this theory remains helpful by recognizing that the policy process includes periods of change and describing how they happen (Smith & Larimer, 2013).

Advocacy Coalition Framework

The advocacy coalition framework (ACF) also attempts to account for a nonlinear conception of the policymaking process. A rather recently conceptualized framework (circa the late 1980s), the ACF recognizes that public policy development is a complex process involving a multitude of individuals. At the core of the ACF is the notion of policy subsystems comprised of stakeholders that specialize in a particular policy area. The specialization is necessary to influence policy given the breadth and complexity of most public policies. Stakeholders in a policy subsystem could include agency officials, legislators, policy analysts, interest group leaders, journalists, and researchers (Sabatier & Weible, 2007). Smith and Larimer (2013) explain that "at the heart of ACF are core beliefs, how coalitions organize around such beliefs, and how these belief systems coordinate activity among coalition members to seek policy change" (p. 79).

Beyond nonlinearity, a central difference between the ACF and the rational conception of the policy process described at the outset of this chapter is that the ACF assumes individuals in the policy subsystem can have altruistic motives guided by policy core beliefs rather than purely self-interested motives (Sabatier & Weible, 2007). Members of a policy subsystem organize into coalitions to advocate for their policy beliefs. Coalitions are useful to organize the many stakeholders involved in the policy subsystem, and they can either be strong or weak. Strong coalitions tend to operate under a shared plan, whereas weak coalitions may simply monitor events and/or coordinate needed responses (Sabatier & Weible, 2007).

The beliefs around which coalitions form include "deep core beliefs" that are broad and encompass assumptions about human nature and the proper role of government. On a secondary level, beliefs focus on the policy core (Sabatier & Weible, 2007). For example, an advocacy coalition has formed around school vouchers based on the deep core belief that the market economy should apply to government functions and the policy core belief that providing students with vouchers to choose their school will improve educational outcomes.

The ACF is a long-term policy process evaluation instrument; experts recommended analyzing coalitions over 10 years or more (Smith & Larimer, 2013). This is because researchers find that policy subsystems tend to be very stable over time given relationships between members of the policy subsystem. This does not mean that beliefs or preferences of coalitions always remain the same. Policy learning allows coalitions to continually monitor and adapt to changes in the environment and revise policy preferences (Smith & Larimer, 2013).

The ACF helps researchers conceptualize policy groups. DeBray-Pelot, Lubiensky, and Scott (2007) used the ACF to map the landscape of school choice interest groups. They found that traditional conceptions of the political right and left did not exactly align to school choice coalitions, as coalitions for and against school choice spanned both sides of the political aisle.

Policy Diffusion

The theories discussed previously highlight factors within a state or other governmental entity that may affect policy adoption and development. There is also the possibility that factors external to the governmental entity contribute to the policy agenda. For example, it often seems that there are policy "trends" that move across states. Policy diffusion helps to explain how policies spread from state to state (Berry & Berry, 2007). While most of the diffusion research focuses on state-to-state diffusion, the principles could likely be applicable among regions or districts. There are several different models of policy diffusion.

The national interaction model suggests that states learn from each other through communication networks among state officials (Berry & Berry, 2007). These networks can be facilitated by associations such as the National Governors Association, the National Council of State Legislatures, conferences such as the Education Commission of the States' annual meeting, or other intermediaries such as think tanks or nonprofits that convene policymakers. The theory holds that the probability that a state will adopt a policy is proportional to the number of interactions policy leaders have with states that have already adopted the policy. It might sound a bit like a peer pressure model, but it makes sense that if policymakers are interacting with other state policymakers who have adopted a certain policy, they may simply be learning more about the policy. As practical as it sounds, a potential limitation of this theory is that it treats all states uniformly and as equally likely to adopt a policy, when in reality states have very different contexts (Berry & Berry, 2007).

The regional diffusion model is much like the national interaction model, but it presumes that state leaders learn the most from activity in states geographically closest to them, as perhaps states in proximity to each other share similar characteristics (Berry & Berry, 2007) and/or compete with each other as they work toward enhancing economic development. Certainly the possibility for this exists through regional education compacts such as the Western Interstate Compact for Higher Education (WICHE) and the Southern Regional Education Board (SREB), among others. Each regional compact serves a set of regional states and focuses on K–12 and/or higher educational issues. Along with issuing state comparison data and developing policy briefs, regional education compacts also play a networking function. For example, SREB hosts annual policymaker meetings and legislative conferences. Potentially, the regional diffusion model is limited by advanced technology and data systems, which now allow states to compare themselves to similar states outside of the region and learn how these states are addressing similar issues.

The leader-laggard diffusion model posits that some states are recognized as pioneers in a certain policy area, and other states emulate them (Berry & Berry, 2007). This model assumes that states emulate other states because of enhanced knowledge, not necessarily for competitive reasons (Berry & Berry, 2007). Tennessee could be considered a leader state in higher education, given its 1979 implementation of the first higher education performance-funding model, which calculated funding for higher education based, in part, on predefined metrics rather than student enrollment. Now, 30 states have some sort of performance-funding model, and several of them have looked to Tennessee for guidance. The likely rationale for state adoption of these new formulas after consulting with Tennessee may not be to compete with Tennessee, but to generate improved higher education outcomes given perceptions of Tennessee's success.

Finally, the vertical influence model recognizes the influence one level of government may have on another, such as the influence the federal government may have on states (Berry & Berry, 2007). There are three potential ways that states would gain knowledge about and/or adopt policies through this model. First, as with the previous examples, states could emulate federal policies that are producing outcomes similar to those the state seeks. Second, the federal government could mandate state adoption of a policy, such as integrated public schools. Finally, the federal government may incentivize state policy adoption through provision of funding, much like the Obama administration did through the Race to the Top (RTTT) grant competition in which states agreed to adopt policies concerning teacher evaluation, charter schools, learning standards, and more, in exchange for a chance to earn millions of dollars.

McLendon and Cohen-Vogel (2008) note that most likely, both internal (contextual factors) and external (diffusion) determinants play a role in state policy adoption. A study by McLendon, Hearn, and Deaton (2006) on state adoption of higher education policy innovations supports this suggestion. The authors examined how and when state governments adopted new performance accountability policies for higher education between the years 1979 and 2002. They found that diffusion through regional networks did not make it more likely that a state would adopt a higher education performance-funding formula (McLendon et al., 2006). Rather, the number of Republicans in the legislature and the type of state higher education governing body influenced whether a state would adopt a performance-funding model (McLendon et al., 2006). So, although states may learn about a policy through regional or national networks, what actually compels them to adopt a particular policy may rely more on internal determinants.

Conclusion

Many scholars spend careers developing and investigating policy process theories. This chapter is but a brief overview of some of the more relevant policy theories to provide the reader some context for why a policy may develop the way it does. Interested citizens and education stakeholders alike may wonder why this or that simple solution is not implemented to solve the nation's educational problems. Policy theories help to explain that the process is usually not simple. Myriad actors, problems, and solutions can be combined in an exponential number of ways to create policies. It may be a miracle that they are all ever combined in just the right way at just the right time to actually produce a policy. Whether the policy is effective is another issue, and this is the focus of those who conduct program and/or policy evaluations. Many university-based public administration degree programs offer at least one course on such evaluation techniques. Chapter 7 on the development and uses of educational research will examine in more depth how policy analysis is used in policy development and, more generally, will look at the role of information in the policy development process.

For Further Information

- The Policy Agendas Project is a website hosted by the University of Texas at Austin that collects and organizes data from various sources to trace changes in the national policy agenda and public policy outcomes since the mid-1940s: www.policyagendas.org/
- Paul Sabatier's *Theories of the Policy Process* (2nd ed.) and Kevin Smith and Christopher Larimer's *The Public Policy Theory Primer* (2nd ed.) both offer concise and clear explanations of many pertinent public policy theories.

Note

1. The author would like to acknowledge Denisa Gandara, clinical assistant professor of education at Southern Methodist University and Ph.D. candidate at the University of Georgia's Institute of Higher Education, for her insightful comments and additions to this chapter. Any errors or omissions are those of the author.

References

Berry, F., & Berry, W. (2007). Innovation and diffusion models in policy research. In P. Sabatier (Ed.), *Theories of the policy process* (2nd ed., pp. 223–260). Boulder, CO: Westview Press.

Cohen, M., March, J., & Olsen, J. (1972). A garbage can model of organizational choice. *Administrative Science Quarterly, 17*(March), 1–25.

DeBray-Pelot, E., Lubiensky, C., & Scott, J. (2007). The institutional landscape of interest group politics and school choice. *Peabody Journal of Education, 82*(2), 204–230.

Doyle, W., & Kirst, M. (2015). Explaining policy change in K–12 and higher education. In M. Stevens & M. Kirst (Eds.), *The changing ecology of higher education* (pp. 190–209). Palo Alto, CA: Stanford University Press.

Kingdon, J. (2011). *Agendas, alternatives, and public policies* (2nd ed.). Boston, MA: Longman.

McDonnell, L., & Weatherford, M. S. (2013). Evidence use and the common core state standards movement: From problem definition to policy adoption. *American Journal of Education, 120*, 1–25.

McLendon, M., & Cohen-Vogel, L. (2008). Understanding education policy change in the American states: Lessons from political science. In B. Cooper, J. Cibulka, & L. Fusarelli (Eds.), *Handbook of education politics and policy* (pp. 30–51). New York, NY: Routledge.

McLendon, M., Hearn, J., & Deaton, R., (2006). Called to account: Analyzing the origins and spread of state performance-accountability policies for higher education. *Educational Evaluation and Policy Analysis, 28*(1), 1–24.

Mills, M. (2007). Stories of politics and policy: Florida's higher education governance reorganization. *The Journal of Higher Education, 78*(2), 162–187.

Mintrom, M. (1997). Policy entrepreneurs and the diffusion of innovation. *American Journal of Political Science, 41*(3), 738–770.

Ripley, R. (2010). The nature of the policy process. In C. Lovell, T. Larson, D. Dean, & D. Longanecker (Eds.), *ASHE reader on public policy and higher education* (2nd ed., pp. 51–63). Boston, MA: Pearson.

Sabatier, P. (2007). The need for better theories. In P. Sabatier (Ed.), *Theories of the policy process* (2nd ed., pp. 3–13). Boulder, CO: Westview Press.

Sabatier, P., & Weible, C. (2007). The advocacy coalition framework: Innovations and clarifications. In P. Sabatier (Ed.), *Theories of the policy process* (2nd ed., pp. 189–220). Boulder, CO: Westview Press.

Smith, K., & Larimer, C. (2013). *The public policy theory primer* (2nd ed.). Boulder, CO: Westview Press.

True, J., Jones, B., & Baumgartner, F. (2007). Punctuated-equilibrium theory. In P. Sabatier (Ed.), *Theories of the policy process* (2nd ed., pp. 155–187). Boulder, CO: Westview Press.

Part II

THE EDUCATION SECTORS

Chapter 4

Early Childhood Education[1]

Introduction

In a recent survey, 73% of Americans said that early childhood education (generally including children from birth to kindergarten) is extremely or very important to a person's ability to succeed in life. While this percentage seems relatively high, it is less than those who believe high school (95%) and college (77%) are extremely or very important to success (Jones, 2014). However, it appears that calls for high-quality early childhood education are increasing from local, state, and federal governments; Democrats and Republicans; think tanks; and the public. In fact,

> since 2003, states have increased their investment in preschool by more than 200 percent. In 2014, 28 states increased their investments, amounting to more than $1 billion in new state resources dedicated to early education.
>
> (U.S. Department of Education, 2015, p. 5)

Early childhood education is probably one of the most dynamic sectors of public education at this point in time; education for the youngest U.S.

citizens, aged birth to five, has grown to be a very popular policy agenda item over the past five decades, particularly given emerging research on child development and neuroscience.

Early childhood education became part of the nation's education agenda through President Lyndon B. Johnson's war on poverty and the creation of Head Start, a federal program for low-income preschoolers. Prior to this program, government-funded childcare briefly appeared during World War II, when the government had a need for women to enter the workforce. After the war, it again was thought of as something only poor working women needed and public efforts died down somewhat. Until President Johnson made the needs of the poor a national priority, early childhood education was not a strong policy concern (Lowenstein, 2011). Over the subsequent decades, the policy impetus for early childhood education extended, and perhaps shifted, from the benefits to working women to the benefits conferred upon students who participated in early learning opportunities. This became stronger as the K–12 standards movement appeared and early childhood education was seen as a way to ensure children were ready for kindergarten and further academic work (Lowenstein, 2011). As of 2013, 41.8% of three-year-olds and 67.7% of four-year-olds were enrolled in preschool, and 51% of three- and four-year-olds enrolled in preschool attend a full-day program (National Center for Education Statistics, 2015). Altogether, 12.5 million children under age five are in some type of regular childcare arrangement (Laughlin, 2013). Preschool enrollment differs by income and race. While 64% of three- and four-year-olds in families earning $100,000 or more participate in preschool, only 40% of children in households earning $20,000 or below do (Education Week Research Center, 2015). Just over half of Asian, Black, and White three- and four-year-olds participate in preschool, whereas just under 40% of Hispanic children do (Education Week Research Center, 2015). Early childhood education is becoming a larger and more foundational component of the educational pipeline; therefore, it is important to understand its many components.

First, there are several different programs and goals that collectively make up the early childhood education sphere. *Pre-kindergarten* usually refers specifically to state-funded educational programs for four- and sometimes three-year-olds. *Head Start* is a federal program that provides comprehensive (health, emotional, family, education) services for three- and four-year olds. *Childcare* often refers to the placement of a child from birth to school age in some type of care arrangement (home, day care, preschool) on a fee basis; childcare may have an educational component, but it is primarily used as a safe, social environment for children whose parents work outside of the home. In many cases, a single facility or school will house one or more of these programs both for the convenience of parents looking for options and for facility operators to generate enough income to stay afloat. Coordinating funding streams and quality assessments for facilities that braid together many of these programs can prove challenging, and this will be addressed throughout this chapter.

Governance

Governance of early childhood education is complex and fragmented. What initially started as primarily a private market sector has seen the continued expansion of public participation—first with the federal government and now with recent explosion of state government efforts. The fragmentation has spawned efforts to coordinate the variety of federal, state, and local programs affecting the nation's youngest children, because

> [a] single child might receive services through a federally funded home-visiting program as an infant; day-care services paid for by a different federal funding stream as a toddler; a state, federal, or privately financed preschool at age 4; and a state-funded public education on entering kindergarten.
>
> (Samuels, 2015, p. 2)

This section will provide an overview of historical and current early childhood education governance structures. Because Head Start is integral to the federal government's governance role, it is addressed here.

Federal

In 1965, early childhood education appeared on the national policy agenda through President Johnson's Head Start program. The program's original purpose was to break the cycle of poverty through interventions with low-income families and children. The 1965 report recommending Head Start and authored by a committee of education experts, noted that "during these years the creation of learning patterns, emotional development and the formation of individual expectations and aspirations take place at a very rapid pace" (U.S. Department of Health, Education, and Welfare, 1965, p. 1). The committee met over six weeks during the summer of 1965 and initially recommended that Head Start begin as a summer program. Sargent Shriver, President Johnson's chief adviser on the war on poverty, feared that Head Start would become merely an experiment, and he successfully pushed for full implementation rather than just a summer program (C. Samuels, 2014). Although education was one of the key components of the program, Head Start was originally housed in the U.S. Office of Economic Opportunity before moving briefly to the Department of Health, Education, and Welfare, and finally to the Department of Health and Human Services, where it remains today. The formal reason for not placing Head Start with other education programs was that the program included services in addition to education, such as health care and social services. The other, and perhaps more influential, reason was a general loss of confidence at the time in the efficacy of public education programs (Rose, 2007). The consternation over effective governance of K–12 education also led to the creation of separate governance structures for higher education, as will be discussed in Chapter 6. In 1995, the Head Start program was further expanded with the addition of Early Head Start, which serves children less than three years of age and pregnant women (C. Samuels, 2014).

To date, Head Start has served more than 31 million infants, toddlers, and young children (C. Samuels, 2014). Forty-seven percent of these children are four years old, 35% are three years old, and the remainder are between birth and two years old (C. Samuels, 2014). Students participating in the Head Start program are diverse: 42% of students are White, 29% are Black, 9% are biracial, 4% are American Indian/Alaska Native, 2% are Asian, and 13% identified as "other." Sixty-three percent of Head Start students are non-Hispanic and 37% are of Hispanic or Latino origin (U.S. Department of Health and Human Services, 2014). Eligibility criteria continue to include the age of the child and family income. To be eligible for services, a family must meet federal poverty guidelines. Children in all states and territories are offered Head Start programs through local providers vetted by the federal Head Start office. The program currently serves 1 million children through 1,700 local grantees at a federal cost of $8 billion per year (C. Samuels, 2014). States do not have any responsibility for administering Head Start programs except to ensure coordination with other state early childhood programs. Head Start programs are center based, and Early Head Start programs are center or home based. Students may attend four or five days per week, depending on the program structure. Nearly half of Head Start preschoolers go to a center five days per week for over six hours per day (U.S. Department of Health and Human Services, 2014). In fiscal year 2013, Head Start provided services related to job training and adult education to 24% of students' families. The program employs about a quarter million individuals (U.S. Department of Health and Human Services, 2014).

Since the inception of the Head Start program, many policymakers have asked whether the program "works": Does it increase academic, emotional, and social outcomes for students during the program and over time? Evaluations have taken place throughout Head Start's 50-year history. Studies on early childhood education as a whole will be explored later in this chapter, but a few Head Start–specific studies are noted here. In 1969, the Office of Economic Opportunity, Head Start's first governmental administering agency, commissioned a study that showed overall poor results. "In sum, the Head Start children can not be said to be appreciably different from their peers in the elementary grades who did not attend Head Start in most aspects of cognitive and affective development measured in this study, with the exception of the slight but nonetheless significant superiority of full-year Head Start children on certain measures of cognitive development" (Westinghouse Learning Corporation, 1969, p. 8). The study also found that Head Start summer-only programs had no impact.

An Early Head Start research and evaluation project started in the late 1990s used a randomized control trial in 17 program sites with 3,001 family participants. Authors found that at the end of the program (when children were three years old), benefits were evident, but modest. Two years later, positive effects continued regarding children's social-emotional outcomes, parenting, and parent well-being. Children who took part in the Early Head Start program followed by another formal early childhood program such as Head Start, pre-K, or center-based childcare had the best outcomes (Vogel, Xue, Moiduddin, Kisker, & Carlson, 2010). When children were studied again in fifth grade, positive impacts on their social-emotional development had continued and were higher for African-American children (Vogel et al., 2010).

A national Head Start Impact Study randomly selected 5,000 three- and four-year-olds in 84 Head Start programs. Data collection began in 2002 and eventually found

> modest to moderate positive impacts after one year of the Head Start program for both 3- and 4-year olds and across most child outcome areas assessed—language, early pre-reading skills, and health. . . . However, the effects found at the end of the Head Start year for the full sample largely disappeared by the end of first grade, with some exceptions.
> (Advisory Committee on Head Start Research and Evaluation, 2012, p. 27)

So, while there are some demonstrated impacts on kindergarten readiness and other socioemotional factors, long-term academic impacts are not conclusive.

Rather than scale back the program based on less-than-optimal performance, federal officials have instead worked to improve the program by frequently strengthening program standards and placing more focus on the academic portion of the program. In 2011, the Department of Health and Human Services adopted new rules requiring Head Start programs not meeting quality benchmarks to reapply for their grants. In 2014, 86 programs had to reapply (U.S. Department of Education, 2015). Most recently, President Obama called for higher early learning program standards in order to improve achievement results (C. Samuels, 2014). The call was timed just as the Head Start office released new research showing mediocre student impacts and the president was preparing to expand his investment in early learning through the Race to the Top Early Learning Challenge (C. Samuels, 2014). With any type of large policy program, there is always a tension between providing sufficient guidelines to ensure fidelity of implementation for optimal outcomes and overburdening fund recipients with too many regulations. Since the inception of Head Start, it seems that most policymakers err on the side of increasing program criteria in the hopes of increasing program effectiveness.

The most recent presidential administration has been very vocal and active regarding the importance of early childhood education. President Obama has couched his support for these policies as assistance for the middle class (U.S. Department of Education, 2013) and as important for regaining the U.S.'s international position regarding education. Among other nations, the U.S. ranks 25th in enrollment of four-year-olds in early learning programs; "fewer than 3 in 10 four-year-olds are enrolled in high-quality preschool programs" (U.S. Department of Education, 2013). In the first years of his administration, President Obama dedicated funding to increase U.S. rates of attendance in high-quality preschool programs. From 2011 to 2013, he awarded between $30 million and $75 million each to 20 states through the Race to the Top Early Learning Challenge, which incentivizes improvement in state early childhood education systems. Grantees are measured on performance metrics related to quality rating and improvement systems (to be discussed in depth later in this chapter). President Obama's 2013 state of the union address focused on creating "a continuum of high-quality early learning for a child—beginning at birth and continuing to age 5" (The White House, 2013) and incentivizing full-day kindergarten for all students. He also started the Invest in US program in December 2014, aimed at creating a coalition of corporate and philanthropic support for early childhood education. Most recently, President Obama initiated two programs to increase quality of and access to state early childhood education programs. The first was the Early Learning Challenge grants noted above awarded to 20 states (half of the applicant pool) in December 2014. States eligible for funding had to have high program standards, the ability to link preschool data with K–12 data, and early learning standards. The U.S. Department of Education found that

> states have used [those] funds to improve early childhood workforce preparation and training; strengthen health services and family engagement; link early childhood and K–12 data systems to learn more about how children's early learning experiences impact school success; and ensure that parents have information about high-quality early learning programs in their communities.
>
> (U.S. Department of Education, 2015, p.6)

The second program, Preschool Development Grants, awarded grants to 18 states to expand the number of children in high-quality preschool programs in high-need communities over four years (U.S. Department of Education, 2015). President Obama's FY2016 budget proposal requests increases in funding for Head Start and Early Head Start—Child Care Partnerships. These programs are part of the president's goal to enroll an additional six million children in high-quality preschool programs (Mongeau, 2014). Ostensibly, the programs noted above are geared to incentivize states to help the nation reach that goal. So, even though the federal government operates an extensive early childhood education program for low-income students (through funding to local providers), it still incentivizes states to expand their own preschool programs.

Recent publications from the U.S. Department of Education urge preschool for all and seek for it to be included in the upcoming federal Elementary and Secondary Education Act reauthorization (see Chapter 5 for more information on ESEA). This would certainly change the status of preschool from an "add-on" to K–12 education to more of an expectation. This seems to be the direction the current presidential administration is going; the U.S. Department of Education cites an "unmet need" in that 60% of four-year-olds do not have access to publicly funded preschool programs (U.S. Department of Education, 2015), signaling a shift to policy prioritization for formal, center-based programs over home-based or parental care for young children.

State

Early childhood education has become an increasingly popular state policy and political topic. In 2014, 23 out of 43 gubernatorial state of the state speeches noted the importance of early childhood education (National Women's Law Center, 2014). Traditionally, state of the state speeches are prime real estate for publicizing policy priorities across a gamut of areas such as health, safety, economic development, and education. Therefore, it is quite striking that over half of these speeches contained exhortations about early childhood education. Further, it appears to be a bipartisan issue, as 13 of the 23 speeches were from Democrats and 10 were from Republicans. The partisan divide was evident, however, in advocacy for targeted versus universal pre-K. Democrats referenced universal pre-K (enrollment without regard to need) and

Republicans referenced targeted pre-K (traditionally targeted to need). Five governors boasted of their federal Race to the Top Early Learning Challenge awards, 16 governors advocated for expanding state pre-K programs, and 2 governors called for raising pre-K standards (National Women's Law Center, 2014). A recent study of 37 state of the state speeches in 2015 (those that occurred at the time of the study) found that 11 governors called for funding to develop or expand preschool and kindergarten programs, especially for low-income families (Aragon & Rowland, 2015).

State policy and monetary support for early learning gained traction in the 1980s, when research touting its long-term positive effects was published and intersected with the public's growing demand for education reform (Rose, 2007). Today, seven states (Florida, Georgia, Illinois, Iowa, New York, Oklahoma, West Virginia) have committed to serving all four-year-olds in pre-K. Illinois is the only state that has committed to serving all three- and four-year-olds (Hustedt & Barnett, 2011). Only eight states have no state-funded preschool program (Samuels, 2015). In 2014, 40 states and the District of Columbia allocated $5.6 billion to fund pre-K spots for 1.3 million three- and four-year-olds (Daily, 2014). When combined with various other funding sources for state pre-K programs (e.g., federal and local contributions), states spend, on average, $4,629 per child enrolled in pre-K (Barnett, Carolan, Squires, & Clarke Brown, 2013). Some experts believe this is woefully below the amount needed to meet program quality benchmarks (Barnett et al., 2013). Spending per child varies widely among states. The top funder is the District of Columbia at $16,853 per child, second is Connecticut at $12,184 per child, and the lowest state is South Carolina at $1,300 per child (Barnett et al., 2013).

States administer and govern their early childhood education programs in a variety of ways. As noted previously in this chapter, there are several programs that touch on the health, safety, and educational needs of the state's youngest citizens, and sometimes the programs overlap services. Not until the 1980s did states begin to focus on coordinating the work of the various programs. Since the mid-2000s, states have taken more strategic actions to align administrative authority for major programs (Regenstein & Lipper, 2013). Regenstein and Lipper (2013) outline three current types of state early childhood services governance. The first is coordination among relevant state agencies, "where administrative authority is vested in multiple agencies that are expected to collaborate with each other" (p. 2). Most states use this manner of governance. In some states the governor's office carries out the coordinating role among agencies, while in others, agencies establish a memorandum of understanding between them. At the very least, almost all states have an early childhood advisory council as required by the Head Start Act. The second manner of governance is consolidation, "in which multiple programs are administered by the same agency, particularly state education agencies" (Regenstein & Lipper, 2013, p. 2). Finally, states may create a new agency to focus on early education and care. Three states (Georgia, Massachusetts, and Washington) utilize this model (Regenstein & Lipper, 2013).

A growing amount of state resources are directed toward early childhood education, and the numbers of children served continue to grow. One way in which the numbers grow is in terms of access to pre-K. As noted previously, there are differing political viewpoints on whether pre-K should be open to all three- and four-year olds in the state (universal) or whether there should be income-based entry requirements (targeted). Thirty-one state programs currently have an income requirement (Barnett et al., 2013). Chester Finn, Jr., former leader of the Fordham Institute and U.S. Department of Education official, summarizes the key arguments against universal pre-K. First he asks, why entrust an already battered public bureaucracy to handle what the market is already supporting? He notes that there is an

> extensive, complex, and vibrant market in preschool and daycare. . . . To layer a new, publicly financed, universal program on top of all this would be a costly and unnecessary windfall for millions of households and be too clumsy and standardized.
>
> (Finn, 2010, p. 12)

In other words, universal pre-K unjustly enriches those who can already pay for quality early learning experiences. Finn also argues that the resources spent on all children through universal pre-K would be better spent on providing extremely high-quality learning opportunities to those students who really need them. He claims universal pre-K is a political tactic—politicians promote it to garner more voters—saying, "the bona fide interests of disadvantaged children are being subordinated to the politics of getting something enacted" (p. 13). The argument of enacting education policy to pander to voters also arises when examining state postsecondary merit aid scholarship programs, as we will see later in this book.

On the flip side, researchers Jason Hustedt and W. Steven Barnett (2011) detail the advantages of universal pre-K. They note that it is difficult to target disadvantaged students because family financial status may frequently change, thereby causing a "revolving door" in and out of pre-K programs. Hustedt and Barnett also cite research demonstrating greater positive impacts on disadvantaged students when more advantaged students are included in pre-K classrooms. They believe these advantages accrue to the higher income students as well. This argument is similar to the one made in postsecondary education related to the benefits of a diverse student body for all students. Finally, Hustedt and Barnett acknowledge the practical and political reality that Finn (2010) cautions against—universal pre-K is more palatable to voters. There are myriad other policy issues related to state pre-K programs, but these will be addressed later, as they cross both federal and state programs.

Finance

Funding streams for early childhood education, like K–12 and higher education programs, are complex. A mixture of federal, state, local, and private funding supports early childhood programs. And within each of the public "buckets" of funding are several smaller sources of funding, each with its own attached regulations, creating a tangled web. As Hustedt and Barnett (2011) explain:

> Different funding streams for public preschool programs tend not to be coordinated with each other. As a result, these funding streams may be viewed as separate silos. Each federal, state, or local funding silo comes with its own requirements, and to the extent that preschool providers blend or braid funds from different sources to create a single classroom, they must coordinate across the (sometimes conflicting) regulations associated with each silo.
>
> (p. 169)

The authors provide a complementary chart to illustrate their point. Table 4.1 describes the separate funding streams from federal, state, and local sources. In two cases (early childhood special education and state pre-K programs), both federal and state monies are combined to support the program (Hustedt & Barnett, 2011).

Table 4.1 Early Childhood Education Funding Streams

Initiative	Funding source	Administrative agency	Primary goals	Eligibility requirements
Head Start	Federal funds distributed to local grantees	U.S. Dept. of Health and Human Services	Comprehensive child development program for children and their low-income families	Available to families with incomes up to 130% FPL, children ages 3–5 (Head Start) or 0–3 (Early Head Start)
Direct child subsidies	Federal funds with required state matches	U.S. Dept. of Health and Human Services	Child care assistance for low-income working families	Available to working families with incomes up to 85% SMI (CCDF) or who are needy as defined by the state (TANF), children aged between 0 and 13 years
Tax credits	Federal credits against income taxes	U.S. Dept. of the Treasury	Reimbursement or reduction of families' child care expenses	Available to any family with qualifying child care expenses up to age 13, but CDCTC credit amounts are based on income levels
Title I preschool	Federal funds	U.S. Dept. of Education	Various types of education services for disadvantaged children	Available to all preschool-age children in schools where 40% of children are in poverty or to academically at-risk children in schools with lower percentages of children in poverty

Program	Funding	Administering agency	Services	Eligibility
Early Childhood Special Education	Federal and state funds	U.S. Dept. of Education	Special education services for children	Available to all preschool-age children with identified disabilities, or, at states' discretion, developmental delays
State pre-K	State funds, sometimes supplemented with local or federal funds	State Departments of Education, most typically	Education programs for qualifying children, sometimes with additional comprehensive services	Determined at the state level, but often targeted to children at risk
Local programs	Determined at the local level	School districts or other local agencies	Education programs for qualifying children	Determined at the local level

Note: FPL = federal poverty level; SMI = state median income; CDCTC = Child and Dependent Care Tax Credit; CCDF = Child Care and Development Fund; TANF = Temporary Assistance to Needy Families.
Source: Reprinted with permission from Hustedt and Barnett (2011), pp. 170–171.

It is important to highlight the smaller federal programs included in the table because this chapter has not covered them in depth. First, direct federal child subsidies are an annual $8 billion expenditure—$5 billion from the Child Care and Development Fund (CCDF) and $3 billion from Temporary Assistance to Needy Families (TANF). Federal childcare tax credits—which allow eligible families who partake in the program to deduct costs against their taxes—have recently amounted to $3.5 billion annually, benefiting 6.7 million families. Title I federal funds (primarily a K–12 program) provides $400 million for preschool programs in high-need elementary schools. Finally, the Early Childhood Special Education program provides about $374 million in federal funding annually. This particular funding stream requires matching state funds, which have recently totaled $5 billion (Hustedt & Barnett, 2011). These figures are all in addition to requested new funding for federal programs, as described previously, and increasing state expenditures on public early childhood education programs.

For parents with children younger than four years and/or in a state without universal pre-K, quality early childhood care options can be costly. In New York, one of the most expensive childcare states, the cost of infant care as a percentage of median income for a single mother is 56%; for a married couple, it is 16%. The cost of care for a four-year-old is 47% of median income for a single mother and 13% for a married couple. In most cases, the cost of center-based care for two children is more than college tuition (ChildCare Aware of America, 2014).

Major Stakeholders

Early childhood education as a policy field is relatively new compared with K–12 and higher education. On one hand, stakeholders mirror or parallel those found in the other sectors. There are foundations, think tanks, and accreditors that all have some stake in this policy sector and often advocate on behalf of these issues. On the other hand, there are also the parents who not only see early childhood education as an educational and social/emotional benefit for their child, but also see it as a work support (for those parents who work outside of the home). It could be argued that K–12 is also a work support, but culture (and the courts) have long seen K–12 education as a requirement while early childhood education has long been thought of as optional. In addition, K–12 and potentially higher education sectors could be seen as stakeholders in early childhood education, as research increasingly indicates how early learning opportunities affect later academic success. More will be said on that in Chapter 8, which focuses on collaboration between the sectors.

This section will focus on two groups, advocacy organizations and research organizations, because they are very active in this sector and contribute a good deal of information to the ongoing debate around early childhood public policy.

Perhaps the largest advocacy organization is the National Association for the Education of Young Children (NAEYC). NAEYC focuses on children from birth through age eight (roughly third grade) by connecting practice, policy, and research. The organization's website provides updates on federal policy; resources for local, state, and national advocates; and news items. NAEYC hosts conferences and takes positions on early childhood policy topics. NAEYC is perhaps most well-known for its accreditation functions for preschools and day cares as well as early childhood degree programs.

Another prominent advocacy organization is the Ounce of Prevention Fund, which has worked since 1982 to ensure quality early childhood experiences are available to children from birth through age five. Children born in poverty are a particular focus of the organization. The Ounce of Prevention Fund carries out its mission through research, professional development training to early childhood professionals, lobbying at state and federal levels, and publications. In 2007, the Ounce of Prevention Fund initiated the First Five Years Fund, which focuses solely on advocacy at the federal level. An overarching organization focused on leveraging the collective impact of the funding and advocacy organization in this field is the Alliance for Early Success. The Alliance has a roster of state, national, and funding partners working to advance state policies supporting the health, education, and welfare of children from birth to age eight. Finally, Head Start programs have their own advocacy and research organization—the National Head Start Association—which began in 1973 and represents Head Start program grantees.

Research in all areas of education is important and ongoing. However, advances in science have allowed for groundbreaking research on the brain and childhood development, which directly affects early childhood education policy. For 50 years, the Frank Porter Graham Child Development Institute at the University of North Carolina at Chapel Hill has been a leader in early childhood research. The center undertakes research and evaluation projects at state and national levels. Harvard's Center on the Developing Child was started much more recently, in 2006, but it already has a reputation for innovative scientific research and communication of that research to policymakers.

Major Policy Issues

As with the K–12 and higher education chapters, there are several policy issues within early childhood learning that deserve attention. The few chosen for discussion here are critical to the core policies surrounding early childhood education, and they receive vast amounts of attention. Program efficacy (e.g., "does it work"?), quality standards, and alignment between programs and with other grade levels will be discussed in this section.

Program Efficacy

The billion-dollar question is whether early childhood programs confer sufficient and meaningful benefits to children—and perhaps by extension, to the economy—to justify the expenditure of public funds. Academic researchers, policy analysts, and policymakers continue to hotly debate this issue. Benefits are usually measured in academic, social, and/or economic terms and are assessed in the short and long term. Policymakers and other early childhood advocates often rely on a core set of rigorous studies that show modest to significant benefits from high-quality early learning experiences. Three of the most often cited studies are detailed here.

The High/Scope Perry Preschool Study was started in 1962 with a small sample of African-American three- and four-year-olds who were randomly assigned to a high-quality early learning program or no program at all. Those in the program received daily two and a half hour classes and a weekly one and a half hour home visit from October through May. Child/staff ratios were at or below six to one (Lowenstein, 2011). The Carolina Abecedarian

Project began in 1972 with random assignment of high-risk infants to full-day, year-round preschool. The control group of infants was in home care or another early childhood education setting. Both groups received social services as needed (Lowenstein, 2011). Finally, the Chicago Child-Parent Center study was conducted in the mid-1980s and provided half-day preschool to three- and four-year-olds in a setting with a child/teacher ratio of 17 to 2, parent involvement, home visits, and health services (Lowenstein, 2011). Researcher Amy Lowenstein worked to assess the results of these studies against the rhetoric surrounding early learning benefits. She found that together these studies "suggest that high-quality early education programs can have remarkably long-lasting, positive effects on low-income children's cognitive, academic, and socioemotional functioning" (p. 101). She further states,

> [a] review of the literature on the development effects of child care, Head Start/Early Head Start, and state-funded preschool suggests that early childhood education programs can and do have positive effects on children from both low- and higher-income families, but that these effects typically fade over time.
>
> (p. 107)

However, Lowenstein cautions that most early childhood education programs are not of the high quality found in the study programs. The small staff to child ratios and other provided services, along with small research sample populations, make it difficult to extend these results to the many early childhood programs dotting our national landscape today.

There are two important aspects regarding the effects fading over time. First, while the effects may fade in later school years, adult outcomes such as high school graduation, teen pregnancy, and criminality were positively affected by quality early childhood education, according to a meta-analysis of experimental early childhood education studies (Duncan & Magnuson, 2013). Second, it is difficult to assess later effects of early childhood education given the intervening school years. What happens in first or fifth grade affects a child's learning as well. The "jump start" students receive through early childhood education is something that needs to be built upon year after year.

The other way some researchers assess efficacy is through analyzing the rate of return or return on investment. A study conducted by Harvard scientists found that "ensuring children have positive experiences prior to entering school is likely to lead to better outcomes than remediation programs at a later age, and significant up-front costs can generate a strong return on investment" (Center on the Developing Child, 2007, p. 2). James Heckman, professor of economics at the University of Chicago and Nobel Laureate in Economics, is perhaps one of the best known experts in the economics of human development. He argues, "the rate of return for investments in quality early childhood development for disadvantaged children is 7–10% per annum through better outcomes in education, health, sociability, economic productivity and reduced crime" (Heckman, n.d.). He finds that the investment in early childhood education is more cost effective than investment in later grades and should occur as early in a child's life as possible. A recent study adds additional support for these assertions. North Carolina's early childhood initiatives were found to have an effect in reducing special education placement in later school years. The Smart Start Initiative, which provided comprehensive services for babies up to five years old, reduced special education placement by 10%, while the More at Four program that funds preschool for four-year-olds reduced placement by 32%. Since special education services are more expensive than early childhood education, at least in North Carolina, this provided a cost savings to the state (Muschkin, Ladd, & Dodge, 2015).

Advocates and increasingly more policymakers are calling for greater investments in early childhood education. Emerging research on the importance of early learning activities indicates that the achievement gap may start soon after birth. The environment in which babies and children are cared for has effects on later functioning. For example, extreme household stress caused by poverty or violence can impede the brain's regulation of emotions and other functioning in later years. On the flip side, parents who provide cognitive stimulation for their baby, including talking with their baby and mirroring or responding to the baby's emotions, support the baby's brain development and, consequently, the growing child develops more advanced language skills (Putnam, 2015). Many advocates of early childhood education would like to see high-quality early learning experiences to ensure that all babies and young children receive the kinds of emotional and cognitive support that are so important in the early years and that have later effects on children as students.

Quality Standards

Acknowledgment that only high-quality programs produce significant results spurs the strong policy emphasis on higher standards for program quality. At a minimum, most states have licensing systems for childcare centers (including home day cares), which provide a threshold bar for quality and compliance standards that entities must meet to legally operate (U.S. Department of Health and Human Services, 2011). However, licensing exemptions are common and are frequently provided to family day care facilities with three or fewer children, facilities in public schools, and part-day programs. States vary widely on content of licensing requirements and fidelity of enforcement (U.S. Department of Health and Human Services, 2011).

Thirty-nine states have adopted Quality Rating and Improvement Systems (QRISs) to supplement their licensing systems. The remaining 11 states are in various stages of QRIS planning. These systems provide information about center/program quality to parents and the public and are designed to encourage educational experiences (rather than just care) in early learning programs. According to the QRIS Network, "[a] well designed QRIS provides the following: Quality assurances by creating and aligning program and professional standards and assessing and monitoring how well programs meet those standards." QRISs often assign star ratings to programs and assess the "classroom learning environment, staff training and education, parent involvement, classroom ratios, director leadership and business practices, use of child assessments and developmentally appropriate curricula" (Schaack, Tarrant, Boller, & Tout, 2012, p. 72). Beyond transparency, QRISs can also be used to direct financial and technical assistance to programs (Schaack et al., 2012). While all states are now headed toward implementation of a QRIS, some states were initially hesitant to imprint a government rating on private programs, citing the huge responsibility (and attendant potential liability) for ensuring the ratings were accurate as well as entangling government and market functions.

The National Institute for Early Education Research (NIEER) quality standards are a set of 10 program policies and related benchmarks developed through research on high-quality preschool programs like those reviewed previously. Four of the 10 recommended policies and benchmarks relate to teacher quality. Table 4.2 presents a list of the 10 standards and the number of state preschool programs that meet the benchmark. A majority of states are working toward meeting some or all of these benchmarks as an indication of quality.

Table 4.2 States Meeting the National Institute for Early Education Research Quality Standards

National Institute for Early Education Research Quality Standards	
Standard and benchmark	*Number of states meeting the recommended benchmark[a]*
The state has a comprehensive set of early learning standards	53
Lead teachers must have a bachelor's degree	30
Lead teachers have specialized training in pre-K	45
Assistant teachers have a Child Development Associate (CDA) credential or equivalent	15
Teachers have at least 15 hours per year of in-service training	42
Maximum class size for three- and four-year-olds is 20 students or fewer	45
Staff–child ratio is 1:10 or lower	46
Vision, hearing, health, and at least one other support service are provided to children	36
Meals are provided at least once per day	25
Site visits are conducted at least every five years	32

Source: Adapted from Barnett et al. (2013).
[a] NIEER bases its counts on 53 state programs, as some of the 40 states offering pre-K education offer more than one program.

Accreditation is also a popular mechanism for early childhood programs to signal their quality to parents and the public. Since 1985, NAEYC, one of the most popular accreditation entities, has accredited childcare programs and preschools. More than 6,500 such programs across the nation are now accredited by NAEYC.

One area that permeates all forms of quality improvement is promoting greater professionalism of the teaching staff. Traditionally, early childhood education teachers were not required to hold the same credentials or licensure as K–12 teachers. As the push for higher early learning program standards increased, so did the push for more qualified teachers. In 2007, Head Start revised their guidelines "to mandate that all teachers have an associate's degree and half have a bachelor's degree by 2013" (McCabe & Sipple, 2011, p. e9). Fifty-seven percent of state-funded pre-K programs mandate that lead teachers have at least a bachelor's degree, which is up from 45% in 2001 (Barnett et al., 2013). Perhaps greater credentials and higher pay will help stem the high turnover rate of childcare staff, which is 29.5% per year versus 9.8% for elementary school teachers (Regenstein, Marable, & Britten, 2014).

The child development associate (CDA) credential was developed out of the federal Head Start office and was first awarded in 1975 for professionals other than lead teachers working with early learners. The CDA is based on a set of core competencies and allows recipients to receive certain age-level endorsements or other specializations. To date, over 300,000 professionals have received this nationally transferrable credential. While the push for higher credentials continues, a wage gap remains. On average, childcare workers earn $9.98 per hour, preschool teachers earn $16.61 per hour, and kindergarten teachers earn $34.24 per hour (Center for the Child Care Workforce, 2011). Low salaries may have the effect of limiting the number of high-quality teachers and paraprofessionals choosing to work in early childhood education, especially if kindergarten through third grade positions are higher paying and available.

Mechanisms for ensuring program quality are expanding and overlapping because early childhood programs may be simultaneously licensed, accredited, and quality rated. Federal Head Start programs have a more simple quality regime, as all adhere to the same standards administered by the Department of Health and Human Services. The federal Race to the Top

Early Learning Challenge competitive grant program incentivizes states to develop and adopt quality rating systems that align standards for and include all publicly funded early childhood programs in the state, including Head Start. Further, as state data systems continue to develop and improve, early childhood education programs can move beyond systems that monitor inputs of quality (although those will likely remain important) and move more toward measures of output, including academic and nonacademic skills.

Alignment

Alignment across early childhood education programs and with state K–12 systems is a major point of policy discussion and efforts. Disparate mixes of funding streams and quality standards have already demonstrated a need for alignment across early childhood programs—not only to promote resource efficiency, but also to aid providers in program administration. After more than 50 years of growth and the creation of separate public (federal, state, local) and private early childhood education governance structures, many policymakers and leaders are calling for coordination. The federal government has encouraged states to focus on coordination and alignment through the 2007 reauthorization of Head Start, which required states receiving funds to establish State Advisory Councils on Early Childhood Education and Care (Regenstein, 2013). The recent federal Race to the Top Early Learning Challenge program requires awarded states to enhance coordination. States are also acting without federal incentive. In the last several years, at least three states (Georgia, Massachusetts, Washington) have created new state agencies that focus on early childhood education and care (Kauerz & Kagan, 2012). Recently, Louisiana's chief state school officer, John White, announced a state coordination effort, noting that "our mission is to take a fragmented system of early childhood, with different expectations from one place to the next, and to unify that system so no child falls through the cracks" (D. Samuels, 2014).

Beyond coordination within early childhood education programs, some wonder whether preschool programs would be more effective if they were connected to K–12 governance structures. Certainly, there is much to be gained by aligning preschool learning standards with early elementary grades for a seamless early childhood through third grade continuum. The National Governors Association (2010) recently released a policy brief urging state governors to focus on this alignment, especially given the implementation of new K–12 standards in many states. While most researchers and policymakers appear to be in agreement about the benefits of aligning standards across early learning and K–12, connecting the governance structures is less warmly received. As public early childhood programs were created, they expanded access but also competed with existing private providers. A strong private market in itself is a barrier to full integration of early learning with the public school system. However, some policymakers also feared attaching early childhood education responsibilities to the public school systems because they were generally seen to be ineffectual and unresponsive (Finn, 2010). Further, public schools do not have a history of providing wraparound services (e.g., home visits, health care, social services) to students, which is a core component of high-quality early learning programs (Rose, 2007).

Looking Forward

As the push continues to expand access to and the quality of early childhood education, many questions remain. Can the nation (and its states) afford the type of high-quality programs that result in the greatest academic and socioemotional outcomes? If not, do our leaders have the political wherewithal to reserve government-funded spots in the highest quality programs for the nation's children that need it most? Will it be the new normal for all children to enter some type of formal, center-based program rather than to have parental care for the first five years of life? These and other types of tough questions regarding early learning may be why reauthorization of the federal Head Start Act is stalled in Congress. The act was most recently reauthorized in 2007 and was slated again for 2012, but has still to be acted upon.

Also, will researchers continue to conduct rigorous analyses of early childhood learning and help to clearly identify the program components needed for optimal student outcomes? For instance, Washington, DC, provides funds for 100% of its four-year-olds to attend pre-K (94% of funds come from DC sources and 6% come from federal Head Start funds). The funding levels per child are the highest in the nation (Barnett et al., 2013). However, K–12 achievement in DC is abysmal. This seems like a prime opportunity to research the connection between universal programs, high funding levels, and outcomes. Overall, it appears that the highest quality programs can have an impact on students in the short term and possibly the long term. Yet, the core group of positive studies repeatedly cited by policy leaders and early childhood education advocates as they champion expanding early learning are not often what appears when access is expanded. This explains the multitude of policy and support organizations and foundations working to improve the quality of early learning opportunities. There is cause for optimism when considering program quality, as it is likely that the implementation of higher K–12 learning standards occurring in most states will trickle down to early learning and perhaps cause all educational components of program quality to rise. Further, new developments in neuroscience will shed light on how best to prepare babies and toddlers for learning throughout their lifetimes. Perhaps then, as Regenstein, et al. (2014) note:

> the issue is not whether the early years matter (they do) or whether program quality can affect long-term outcomes (it can). Rather, the issue is whether government can deliver high quality at scale and which children should be the beneficiaries of government spending.
>
> (p. 12)

For Further Information

- The Center on the Developing Child at Harvard University provides information about the impact of adult–child interactions on child development: http://developingchild.harvard.edu
- The National Institute of Early Education Research at Rutgers University, http://nieer.org, and the Frank Porter Graham Child Development Institute at the University of North Carolina at Chapel Hill, http://fpg.unc.edu, provide additional research on early childhood education.
- The Ounce of Prevention Fund, www.theounce.org/, and the First Five Years Fund, www.ffyf.org, are advocacy organizations that provide ample resources on early learning through their websites.

- The Alliance of Early Success organizes state, national, and funding partners to leverage collective action for state early childhood policies: http://earlysuccess.org
- The Office of Head Start in the U.S. Department of Health and Human Services provides a website with a good deal of current and historic information and research on the program: www.acf.hhs.gov/programs/ohs
- The Quality Rating and Improvement System National Learning Network hosts a website with a wealth of information on the QRIS: http://qrisnetwork.org
- Professor and Nobel Laureate James Heckman's website contains his studies on the economic impact of early childhood education: http://heckmanequation.org

Note

1. I would like to extend deep gratitude to Elliot Regenstein, senior vice president for advocacy and policy at the Ounce of Prevention Fund based in Chicago, Illinois, for his careful review and thoughtful critique of earlier versions of this chapter. His comprehensive knowledge of early childhood education policy issues made this chapter exponentially better. Any errors or omissions in this chapter remain those of the author.

References

Advisory Committee on Head Start Research and Evaluation. (2012, August). *Advisory committee of Head Start research and evaluation: Final report.* Retrieved from www.acf.hhs.gov/sites/default/files/opre/eval_final.pdf

Aragon, S., & Rowland, S. (2015, February). *Governors' top education issues: 2015 state of the state addresses.* Retrieved from www.ecs.org/html/newsMedia/docs/PR2.24.15.pdf

Barnett, W., Carolan, M., Squires, J., & Clarke Brown, K. (2013). *The state of preschool 2013: State preschool yearbook.* New Brunswick, NJ: National Institute for Early Education Research.

Center for the Child Care Workforce. (2011). *Wage data: Early childhood workforce hourly wage data.* Retrieved from www.ccw.org/index.php?option=com_content&task=view&id=19&Itemid=48

Center on the Developing Child. (2007, August). *Summary of essential findings: A science-based framework for early childhood policy.* Retrieved from www.developingchild.harvard.edu

ChildCare Aware of America. (2014). *Parents and the high cost of child care*. Retrieved from www.arizonachildcare.org/pdf/2014-child-care-cost-report.pdf

Daily, S. (2014, October). *Initiatives from preschool to third grade: A policymakers' guide*. Retrieved from www.ecs.org/docs/early-learning-primer.pdf

Duncan, G., & Magnuson, K. (2013). Investing in preschool programs. *Journal of Economic Perspectives, 27*(2), 109–132.

Education Week Research Center. (2015, January). Preparing to launch: Early childhood's academic countdown: Early-Childhood Education in the U.S.: An Analysis. *Quality Counts 2015*. www.edweek.org/ew/qc/2015/early-childhood-education-in-the-us.html?intc=EW-QC14-TOC.

Finn, C. (2010). Targeted, not universal preK. *Kappan Magazine, 92*(3), 12–16.

Heckman, J. (n.d.). *The Heckman equation papers*. Retrieved from www.heckman equation.org

Hustedt, J., & Barnett, W. (2011). Financing early childhood education programs: State, federal, and local issues. *Educational Policy, 25*(1), 167–192.

Jones, J. (2014, September 8). *In U.S., 70% favor federal funds to expand pre-K education*. Retrieved from www.gallup.com/poll/175646/favor-federal-funds-expand-pre-education.aspx

Kauerz, K., & Kagan, S. (2012). Governance and early childhood systems: Different forms, similar goals. In S. Kagan & K. Kauerz (Eds.), *Early childhood systems* (pp. 87–103). New York, NY: Teachers College Press.

Laughlin, L. (2013, April). *Who's minding the kids? Child care arrangements: Spring 2011*. Retrieved from www.census.gov/prod/2013pubs/p70-135.pdf

Lowenstein, A. (2011). Early care and education as educational panacea: What do we really know about its effectiveness? *Educational Policy, 25*(1), 92–114.

McCabe, L., & Sipple, J. (2011). Colliding worlds: Practical and political tensions of prekindergarten implementation in public schools. *Educational Policy, 25*(1), e1–e26.

Mongeau, L. (2014, October 6). *Obama calls for preschool enrollment of 6 million by 2020*. Retrieved from http://blogs.edweek.org/edweek/early_years/2014/10/obama_calls_for_6_million_enrolled_in_preschool_by_2020.html

Muschkin, C., Ladd, H., & Dodge, K. (2015). Impact of North Carolina's early childhood initiatives on special education placements in third grade. *Educational Evaluation and Policy Analysis*. Advance online publication. doi:10.3102/0162373714559096

National Center for Education Statistics. (2015). *Digest of education statistics*. Retrieved from http://nces.ed.gov/programs/digest/d14/tables/dt14_202.10.asp

National Governors Association Center for Best Practices. (2010, October). *Building ready states: A governor's guide to supporting a comprehensive, high-quality early childhood state system*. Retrieved from www.nga.org/files/live/sites/NGA/files/pdf/1010GOVSGUIDEEARLYCHILD.PDF

National Women's Law Center. (2014, May). *Governors' 2014 state of the state addresses: Mentions of early care and education*. Retrieved from www.nwlc.org/resource/governors'-2014-state-state-addresses-mentions-early-care-and-education

Putnam, R. (2015). Our kids—The American dream in crisis. New York: Simon & Shuster.

QRIS. National Learning Network. http://qrisnetwork.org/our-framework.

Regenstein, E. (2013, May). *State early childhood advisory councils*. Retrieved from www.buildinitiative.org/WhatsNew/ViewArticle/tabid/96/ArticleId/537/State-Early-Childhood-Advisory-Councils.aspx

Regenstein, E., & Lipper, K. (2013, May). *A framework for choosing a state-level early childhood governance system*. Retrieved from www.buildinitiative.org/Portals/0/Uploads/Documents/Early%20Childhood%20Governance%20for%20Web.pdf

Regenstein, E., Marable, B., & Britten, J. (2014, December 2). *Unlocking the potential of children before Kindergarten entry*. Retrieved from http://edex.s3-us-west-2.amazonaws.com/Regenstein%20Paper-KLM%20(1).pdf

Rose, E. (2007). Where does preschool belong? Preschool policy and public education, 1965-present. In C. Kaestle & Lodewick (Eds.), *To educate a nation: Federal and national strategies of school reform* (pp. 281–304). Lawrence: University Press of Kansas.

Samuels, C. (2014, August 5). Head Start endures, evolves as 50-year milestone nears. Retrieved from www.edweek.org/ew/articles/2014/08/06/37wop-head start.h33.html

Samuels, D. (2014, September 15). Pre-school revamp announced by state officials. Retrieved from www.nola.com/education/index.ssf/2014/09/pre-school_re vamp_announced_by.html

Samuels, C. (2015, January 8). Consensus on early ed. value, but policy questions remain. *Education Week*.

Schaack, D., Tarrant, K., Boller, K., & Tout, K. (2012). Quality rating and improvement systems: Frameworks for early care and education systems change. In S. Kagan & K. Kauerz (Eds.), *Early childhood systems* (pp. 71–86). New York, NY: Teachers College Press.

U.S. Department of Education. (2013, March). *Early learning: America's middle class promise begins early*. Retrieved from www.ed.gov/early-learning

U.S. Department of Education. (2015, April). *A matter of equity: Preschool in America*. Retrieved from www.ed.gov/blog/2015/04/a-matter-of-equity-preschool-in-america/

U.S. Department of Health and Human Services. (2011, November). *Office of Child Care issue brief: A foundation for quality improvement systems: State licensing, preschool, and QRIS program quality standards*. Retrieved from http://qrisnetwork.org/sites/all/files/resources/gscobb/2012-03-19%2012%3A52/Report.pdf

U.S. Department of Health and Human Services. (2014). *Head Start program facts: Fiscal year 2014.* Retrieved from http://eclkc.ohs.acf.hhs.gov/hslc/data/fact sheets/2014-hs-program-factsheet.html

U.S. Department of Health, Education, and Welfare. (1965, February 19). *Recommendations for a Head Start program.* http://eclkc.ohs.acf.hhs.gov/hslc/hs/about/docs/cooke-report.pdf

Vogel, C., Xue, Y., Moiduddin, E., Kisker, E., & Carlson, B. (2010). *Early Head Start children in grade 5: Long-term follow-up of the Early Head Start research and evaluation study sample.* Retrieved from www.acf.hhs.gov/sites/default/files/opre/grade5.pdf

Westinghouse Learning Corporation, Ohio University. *The impact of Head Start: An evaluation of the effects of Head Start on children's cognitive and affective development.* (1969, June). Washington, DC: Office of Economic Opportunity.

The White House. (2013, February 13). *Fact sheet: President Obama's plan for early education for all Americans.* Retrieved from www.whitehouse.gov/the-press-office/2013/02/13/fact-sheet-president-obama-s-plan-early-education-all-americans

Chapter 5

K–12

When people refer to "public education," they are usually referring to kindergarten through 12th grade. There are a few good reasons for this. First, unlike early childhood education or college, state laws make K–12 schooling mandatory for all children in the U.S.[1] Second, with 13 grade levels, it forms the core of the educational pipeline. There are almost 50 million students in K–12 public schools and another 5 million in private schools (National Center for Education Statistics, 2014). From the time of the rural one-room schoolhouses to the present, with sprawling suburban high schools, there has been a constant push by the public and policymakers to increase the quality of K–12 education. At times, this took the form of increasing access to schooling such as for rural students, women, immigrants, and minority students. Other times, the push for greater quality centered on more rigorous learning standards and student expectations. The overall goal is to ensure equity and excellence for all students. This becomes increasingly difficult as the population grows and becomes more diverse.

Greater numbers of students and employees, more variety in student needs, and higher expectations for public schools create complex organizational and political issues that are not as easily solved as some leaders and pundits would have us believe. The current student population provides a good picture of the variety of student needs facing American public schools. In 2001, 38.3% of public school students qualified for the federal free/reduced-price meals program. This program is based on family income. So, a family of four with an annual income of $31,005 in 2014–15 would qualify for free meals, and a family of four with an income of $44,123 would qualify for reduced-price meals. In 2013, the percentage of students qualifying for this program rose to over 50% for the first time, an increase of over 10 percentage points in just 10 years (National Center for Education Statistics, 2015). These numbers vary widely by state; New Hampshire has only 27% of students qualifying for the program, while Mississippi has almost 72% of students qualifying for free or reduced-price meals (National Center for Education Statistics, 2015). Student needs are also manifested in other ways. About 9% of U.S. public school students participate in programs for English language learners. Again, this also varies widely by state, with California having about 23% of students requiring such services and West Virginia having less than 1% of students requiring the same (National Center for Education Statistics, 2015). Finally, about 13% of U.S. public school students require services under the federal Individuals with Disabilities Education Act. These figures do not vary as widely by state, but there are a couple of outliers, with Massachusetts at 17% and Texas at almost 9% (National Center for Education Statistics, 2015). This variance may have more to do with student identification procedures than with population numbers.

The complexity of K–12 education is magnified by the transparency of student performance, given more sophisticated state and local data systems. Student academic achievement can be parsed by racial, ethnic, gender, socioeconomic, or other subgroups. Sophisticated formulas allow statisticians to estimate student learning growth year to year and can calculate a teacher's effect on student learning. States compete with each other in the economic development arena based on the strength of education performance. Data have become important, if not king. And the data usually tell a bleak story. In 2013, just over 80% of high school students graduated (GradNation, 2015). This percentage is rising, but it needs to continue to grow to meet state and national attainment goals. A closer examination of the data reveals gaps between various groups of students. For instance, the graduation rate for low-income students was 15 percentage points less than that of middle- and high-income students. Notably, the gap between Kentucky's low-income students and other students was only 1.4 percentage points. There are also gaps between racial subgroups. Hispanic/Latino students had a graduation rate of 75%, African-American students were at 71%, White students were at 87%, and Asian students were at 89%. Further, "the majority of states consistently graduate 85 percent or more of their general population students, but most states are struggling to graduate even 70 percent of students with disabilities" (GradNation, 2015, p. 7).

Leading up to high school graduation, performance on nationally normed tests is very low. Standardized testing and sophisticated data systems now allow us to compare student progress across districts, states, and countries. Only 34% of fourth grade public school students score "proficient" in reading and/or math on the National Assessment of Education Performance, a test that is administered to students across the nation by the U.S. Department of Education (Education Week Research Center, 2014a). U.S. performance compared to international countries is not any better. According to the latest international tests given to students across several countries, American students are faring poorly. U.S. students place ninth of 42 countries in eighth-grade tests in math and tenth place in eighth-grade science tests. In high school, U.S. students place 17th of 34 economically developed countries in reading literacy, 27th in mathematics, and 20th in science (National Center for Education Statistics, 2015).

The structure of K–12 schooling varies from district to district and state to state. For example, about 4%, or 3,700 public schools, offer a year-round schedule rather than providing the traditional two-month summer break (National Center for Education Statistics, 2014). Often, year-round schools do not offer more instructional days, but rather space out breaks throughout the year. States also have different policies on the number of instructional days and hours required of students. These vary by level of education, as most elementary schools operate fewer hours than secondary schools. Colorado requires the fewest number of days at 160, whereas Kansas requires the most at 186. When examining instructional hours, however, Colorado requires more hours than many other states. Arizona requires the fewest total annual hours at the high school level (720), and Wisconsin requires the most (1,137) (National Center for Education Statistics, 2014).

Clearly, the landscape of K–12 education is complex. The purpose of this chapter is to provide an overview of the existing state of K–12 policy along with emerging issues in order to provide the reader with a base from which to extend research and/or reflective thought. Unlike other treatments of this topic, the chapter does not aim to solve the problems surrounding K–12 education, but instead to provide a clear picture of the landscape to help those who are trying to solve those problems.

Governance

Education is the sole province of states, as it is not covered in the U.S. Constitution. However, that does not prevent the federal government from exercising influence over K–12 education through regulations tied to funding. Further, local school districts within states maintain primary responsibility for providing education services to students through authority delegated from the states. The interplay between federal, state, and local education governance has evolved over time, and while this section will describe the basic legal structure, which has not changed much over time, it will also highlight how the balance of power has shifted among these entities.

There are other ways to conceptualize education governance beyond federalism. These include the nature of control (e.g., public versus private), the degree of centralization, and the placement of education policy issues on larger policy agendas. Jeffrey Henig (2013), a professor of education politics at Columbia University, describes an interesting trend in the evolution of education governance. He suggests that education is moving from single-purpose governance to general-purpose governance. Single-purpose governance is characterized by decision making and policymaking by specialized boards (e.g., local public school boards) and interest groups, while general-purpose governance includes education among a panoply of topics on the agendas of mayors, governors, and presidents and activity from nontraditional education interest groups. Henig (2013) believes the "special status [of education] has been eroding, and that we are witnessing the gradual reabsorption of educational decision making into multilevel, general-purpose government and politics" (p. 3). This may explain why the U.S. is seeing so many more mayors, governors, and presidents becoming heavily involved in education policy.

Local

There are 130,000 public schools in the U.S. governed by 13,500 school districts. While the number of schools has remained relatively stable, the number of school districts has drastically decreased over time. In 1940, there were over 100,000 school districts (National Center for Education Statistics, 2014). This trend represents an emphasis on efficiency as fewer school districts govern more schools. Still, some states such as Texas (1,043 local school boards) and Illinois (892 local school boards) boast numerous local boards (Education Commission of the States, 2014). Not only has the number of school districts decreased, but also the type of district has drastically changed over the past several years. As of 2011, only 73% of all school districts were "traditional." The other 27% were made up largely of charter school local education agencies, regional agencies, and other types of configurations (Education Week Research Center, 2014b).

Modern local school boards are expected to

> establish core beliefs, create the vision, set goals, formulate a theory of action for change, direct and participate in the development of policies, approve policies, allocate resources, oversee policy implementation and the effectiveness of management systems, mediate between the district and the public, and look far into the future.
>
> (McAdams, 2006, p. 9)

This is a lengthy and sophisticated list for the average community citizen elected to the school board, who may or may not have any education and/or leadership experience. Although the scope of these tasks may change depending on the size or location of the school district, the fundamental responsibilities do not. Therefore, basic levels of knowledge, leadership skills, and integrity are important whether a school board member sits in rural North Dakota or urban Philadelphia. The National School Boards Association and various other organizations expend a good deal of effort working to make school boards more "effective." Certainly, school boards are the first place for the buck to stop when there are significant achievement or other problems across a school district. Recently, it appears that in some places public satisfaction with the work of school boards has reached such low levels that control over district schools has eroded. For example, many cities have ceded all or some control over schools to mayors "by giving them greater power in selecting superintendents, selecting school boards, authorizing charter schools, determining the budget, or all of the above"

(Henig, 2013, p. 59). Power was once before in the hands of city leaders, but around the turn of the 20th century, in an effort to depoliticize education, power was instilled in specific-purpose local boards (Henig, 2013). As we move back to greater mayoral and gubernatorial control—as will be discussed further—it seems that perhaps education cannot be depoliticized, and if politicians are going to be held accountable for educational outcomes, they also want some control over them.

Beyond potential public dissatisfaction with local school boards, accreditation agencies seem to be holding local school boards more accountable and are suspending school district accreditation based on poor performance. For example, in just the past few years, AdvancED, parent company of several regional accreditors, placed three Atlanta metro area school boards (Atlanta Public Schools, Clayton County Public Schools, and Dekalb County Public Schools) on probation for governance issues.

State

The state's governor, a state board of education, and a chief state school executive usually carry out state governance of K–12 education. There are a few general configurations of power-sharing among these leaders that vary by whether the governor appoints the chief state school executive and/or the state board (Scudella, 2013). The most popular configuration (14 states) is where the elected governor appoints the state board of education who, in turn, appoints the chief state school executive. Nine states utilize a model where the governor appoints the state board of education and the chief state school executive is elected. Seven states elect both the governor and state board of education, who then appoints the chief state school executive. In 11 states, the governor appoints both the state board and the chief state school executive. Only two states (Minnesota and Wisconsin) operate without a state board of education. Other configurations include a mixed elected/appointed state board and involvement by the legislature in appointing state board members (Scudella, 2013).

The responsibilities and influence of each entity vary by state depending on political context, policy context, history, and individual personalities. However, there are general definitions of what each should do. "In general, most state boards have six legal powers in common. They: (1) establish certification standards for teachers and administrators, (2) establish high school graduation requirements, (3) establish state testing programs, (4) establish standards for accreditation of school districts and teacher and administrator preparation programs, (5) review and approve the budget of the state education agency, and (6) develop rules and regulations for the administration of state programs" (Education Commission of the States, 2015).

State boards of education became popular among states in the 1940s and 1950s as a mechanism to help insulate education from partisan politics, provide for greater citizen representation, allow for greater continuity in educational policy, and protect against abuses of power (Henig, 2013). Some states may assign some of these duties to other boards or agencies. For example, Georgia entrusts the Professional Standards Commission, an agency separate from the state department of education, to establish teacher and leader certification standards and establish standards for accreditation of teacher and administrator preparation programs.

Chief state school executives "are responsible for the general supervision of the state's public education system . . . [they lead] the state education agency and direct activities of the agency's professional staff in regulating and supporting the state's public schools" (Education Commission of the States, 2014). Although most of these individuals report to the state board of education, they must also work with governors, legislatures, and other agency leaders to accomplish their goals. This becomes a more difficult job when the chief state school executive is elected, because he/she then has an individual platform and campaign promises to deliver upon. In the 14 states where the chief state school executive is elected, governors may set up separate agencies or offices to carry out educational programs if the governor and chief state school executive do not share agendas.

Arguably, the governors' role in education is increasing based on a confluence of several contemporary factors, including increased state accountability from federal programs (e.g., No Child Left Behind legislation of 2001), mounting public dissatisfaction with education and assignment of responsibility to governors, and the trending gubernatorial view of education as an economic development tool. Henig (2013) argues that gubernatorial power over education has been increasing for several decades and that the rise of "education governors" started in the 1950s and escalated after 1995; notably, from 1995 to 2009, 60% of governors' biographies on the National Governors Association website mentioned a substantive K–12 interest. Shober (2012) also believes that gubernatorial interest in and influence over education are increasing, particularly from a fiscal angle. Given that K–12 education is such a large part, if not the largest part, of the state's budget, "the financial pressures of the last decade have made state education budgets the cornerstone of state budget politics, and thus a problem no governor can avoid" (Shober, 2012, p. 560). Yet, it is important to note that the power and influence of the governor also varies by state depending on "whether the governor's party controls the legislature, how strong the governor is within his or her own party, the professionalism of the legislature, the existence and mobilization of supporting interest groups, and the ambition of the governor's objectives" (Henig, 2013, p. 43).

Federal

As noted previously, the federal government has no constitutional role regarding the education of the nation's citizens; however, it has an increasingly growing influence on education policy. This is likely the result of several factors. One is the president's use of the bully pulpit to advocate for increased education quality. Mentions of education in state of the union speeches and inclusion of education in the federal budget are now considered typical presidential policy activities. Second, federal and state leaders seem to generally agree on the need for increased educational rigor and achievement. While there may not be total agreement on ways to achieve this, state leaders can see the benefits in allowing the federal government to support their work. The third factor is the ability of the federal government to leverage funding for specific policies and performance in furtherance of presidents' aims. This is not unique to President Obama, although it could be argued that federal leverage has significantly increased during his terms in office. Whether federal government activity in K–12 education is an overreach, unconstitutional, and/or supportive of state aims is beyond the scope of this book and is treated quite frequently by other policy observers. Therefore, this section will focus on *how* the federal government is currently affecting education governance rather than passing a judgment on its actions.

While, theoretically, it could be said that the president coordinates all federal policy by establishing policy priorities, budgeting funds, and directing agencies to implement such policies, a long-time federal education policy official and observer notes that

> we, as a nation, do not have a national education policy, though most people assume that we do. Instead we have a hodgepodge of federal laws, executive branch policy decisions, regulations, and incentives that have accumulated like so many geological layers since the passage of the National Defense Education Act in 1958.
>
> (Cross, 2014, p. 167)

Still, that hodgepodge of policies seems to be based on similar themes, particularly the need for greater equity and excellence in education. In fact, Cross (2014) argues that federal activity in education has been "instrumental in bringing attention to groups of students who were being left in the shadows in many states and communities" (p. 169), including ethnic and racial minority students, English language learners, and students with disabilities. Certainly, President George W. Bush's No Child Left Behind Act (NCLB) of 2001 focused on ensuring that all subgroups of students (including those mentioned) were proficient in reading and math.

President Obama is continuing the emphasis on "all" students through exhortations to collect and disaggregate student achievement data while simultaneously urging increased quality in learning standards, education professionals, and achievement. His most notable policy/program is the RTTT competitive grant program authorized as part of 2009's American Recovery and Reinvestment Act. Initially, the program offered grants to states to shape K–12 education, but then ancillary RTTT programs offered grants to school districts and for state early childhood learning programs. Application for RTTT funding was completely voluntary, but it came at a time when states found themselves strapped for cash. Perhaps that was the reason 40 states and the District of Columbia applied for a part of the $4 billion in funding, or perhaps the requirements of the grant proposal lined up with what the majority of states were already doing or planned to do. Either way, the requirements for states seeking funding were significant and have permeated other presidential initiatives since 2009. These include:

- Adopting standards and assessments that prepare students to succeed in college and the workplace and to compete in the global economy
- Building data systems that measure student growth and success and inform teachers and principals about how they can improve instruction
- Recruiting, developing, rewarding, and retaining effective teachers and principals, especially where they are needed most
- Turning around the lowest-achieving schools.

Eighteen states were awarded funding and are still involved in some phase of implementation, so the efficacy of RTTT in meeting the president's and states' goals is still undetermined. However, several states have been finding difficulty in developing and implementing new teacher evaluation systems, and there has been some backpedaling on implementation of new standards and assessments, as will be discussed later in this chapter. So, while some argue that RTTT has "arguably become the most visible and celebrated school reform effort in American history" (Henig, 2013, p. 57, quoting Frederick Hess), its overall impact is unclear.

Another major avenue for federal impact on K–12 education is through the Elementary and Secondary Education Act (ESEA) initially proposed and signed by President Lyndon Johnson in 1965 as part of his Great Society programs. Traditionally, this program focused on providing school funding to serve low-income students. This remains part of the current iteration of the legislation, the No Child Left Behind Act, but it was substantially expanded to affect most aspects of K–12 education. No Child Left Behind was the most recent reauthorization of ESEA. The act was due for reauthorization in 2007, but presidents (both Bush and Obama) and Congress have not been able to come to an agreement on a new version. As NCLB stands now, states must collect and disaggregate student achievement data on standardized tests each year. This data is then used for accountability purposes at school, district, and state levels. Failure to meet adequate yearly progress goals can result in sanctions that range from opening school choice options to students to loss of federal funding. The ultimate goal of NCLB was for all students to reach "proficiency" (as defined by the state) in reading and math by 2014. As 2014 neared and states still struggled to meet proficiency goals, the Obama administration provided relief with strings attached. In 2012, states had the option to apply to the U.S. Department of Education for waivers from provisions of the NCLB Act. Requirements for obtaining a waiver are listed in detail below, as they are a good window into the Obama administration's stance on K–12 education policy and its potential negotiations on ESEA reauthorization. To receive a waiver, states had to commit to:

- Adopting *college- and career-ready standards* in at least reading/language arts and mathematics, transitioning to and implementing such standards statewide for all students and schools, and developing and administering annual, statewide, aligned, *high-quality assessments*, and corresponding academic achievement standards, that measure *student growth* in at least grades 3–8 and at least once in high school. (p. 1)

- Develop[ing] and implement[ing] a system of differentiated recognition, accountability, and support for all LEAs in the State and for all Title I schools in these LEAs. Those systems must look at student achievement in at least reading/language arts and mathematics for all students and all subgroups of students identified in ESEA section 1111(b)(2)(C)(v)(II); graduation rates for all students and all subgroups; and school performance and progress over time, including the performance and progress of all subgroups. (p. 2)

- Develop[ing], adopt[ing], pilot[ing], and implement[ing], with the involvement of teachers and principals, teacher and principal evaluation and support systems that: (1) will be used for continual improvement of instruction; (2) meaningfully differentiate performance using at least three performance levels; (3) use multiple valid measures in determining performance levels, including as a significant factor data on student growth for all students (including English Learners and students with disabilities), and other measures of professional practice (which may be gathered through multiple formats and sources, such as observations based on rigorous teacher performance standards, teacher portfolios, and student and parent surveys); (4) evaluate teachers and principals on a regular basis; (5) provide clear, timely, and useful feedback, including feedback that identifies needs and guides professional development; and (6) will be used to inform personnel decisions. (p. 3)

- Remov[ing] duplicative and burdensome reporting requirements that have little or no impact on student outcomes. (p. 3)
- Engage diverse stakeholders and communities in the development of its request (pg. 4) (U.S. Department of Education, 2012).

Forty-one states and the District of Columbia earned waivers which expire in 2015 and the U.S. Secretary of Education is currently considering waiver extensions through the 2017–18 school year. Conditions for these waivers are similar to those offered in 2012, but they include updates on state progress thus far under the existing waiver (U.S. Department of Education, 2014a). The Council of Chief State School Officers received this news favorably, and at least one teacher union group, the American Federation of Teachers (AFT), did not. In a case of strange bedfellows, the AFT is joined by House Education and the Workforce Committee Chairman John Kline (R-MN) who issued a statement in response to the waiver extension, noting that

> our K–12 education system is broken and we've learned over the last several years the president's controversial waiver scheme is not the answer. Instead of changing course, the administration is delivering more arbitrary rules, more regulatory burdens, and more confusion.
>
> (J. Kline, 2014)

Balancing Power

Federalism dictates the broad outline of power sharing among local, state, and federal entities, but there are many opportunities for overlap, as outlined previously. With the federal government leveraging its provision of funding to states for increased power over policies, states accepting more responsibility for the performance of schools, and local boards trying to hold on to their traditional purview over education, it gets complicated. The current version of education "reform" seems to disfavor local school boards and schools, as "the new educational executives are seen as more likely than school boards and bureaucracies to give a fair hearing to these various reform ideas by virtue of being less invested in the status quo" (Henig, 2013, p. 69). Governors (as one of the new educational executives) and the state will likely hold on to and/or increase their new power in the foreseeable future as the federal government continues to incent their action (see Cross, 2014; Shober, 2012; Ujifusa, 2014). However, until local school boards are absolved of budgeting district funds, hiring local teachers, and setting the local curriculum, local school districts will continue to exert a tremendous amount of influence over K–12 classrooms (Henig, 2013).

Finance

The governance issues described previously certainly play into the complexities of school finance. In all states, school funding is a mix of state, local, and federal dollars, but the precise mixture varies across states. Most states allocate funding to local school districts through a formula, usually one that "ties distribution of funds to student enrollment and local revenue capacity" (Roza, 2013, p. 39). Ultimately, local school boards are responsible for allocating funding that comes from these sources, but they are restricted by the requirements attached to the funding. Restrictions could include state laws that mandate a certain number of students per teacher, thereby requiring local school boards to hire a set number of teachers. Restrictions also come from requirements attached to federal funding, such as only spending certain dollars on schools with a specific percentage of low-income students. Finally, local community groups, including teachers' unions and businesses, usually have ideas about how their elected school board should allocate funding.

Prior to allocation issues, there is a never-ending argument about the amount of funding local school districts receive. Local school leaders (and/or the groups representing those leaders) complain that the state does not provide enough funding—either the state is not fully funding its formula, or the formula does not reflect the current needs of schools. On the other hand, state leaders must balance budgets, and K–12 is the largest state expenditure. There are likely no state leaders that set out to monetarily starve schools, especially since education is a large factor in a state's economic development strength. Rather, the issue centers on whether state leaders understand what schools need and/or what resources are required to provide desired student achievement results. Further, economic downturns can restrict the state dollars available for school allocation.

Although there are debates about what constitutes the "right" amount of funding, there is a good amount of data to shed light on current levels of funding. The most recent information available from the National Center for Education Statistics shows that the total amount of revenue for public K–12 schools was $600 billion for school year 2011–12. The majority of funding came from state sources (45.2%), while local sources were a close second (44.6%) followed by federal sources (10.2%) (National Center for Education Statistics, 2015). This is drastically different from almost 100 years ago, when the federal government provided less than 1% of K–12 funding, the state provided 16% and local governments provided over 83% (Cross, 2014). Increases in state and federal funding over the years seem to track these entities' increased roles in education governance.

Note that these are national averages, and the amounts/percentages vary by state. For example, only 5.4% of total education revenue in New Jersey is from federal sources, compared to 16.6% in South Dakota. This variation could be due to a couple of factors, including the number or percentage of students who qualify for grant funding (e.g., Title I funding) or the state's decision to apply for certain federal funds (e.g., RTTT). The mixture of state and local funding also differs by state. In California, 56.3% of school funding is from state sources and 31.1% is from local sources. Compare this to Missouri, where 32.0% of funding is from the state and 57.8% of funding is from local revenues (National Center for Education Statistics, 2015).

An important note concerning revenues is how some states try to even the playing field between wealthy and tax-poor school districts. If a portion of school funding is generated from local taxes, the robustness of the local tax base will either help feed or starve school coffers. In an effort to ensure all students have access to a quality education, states often find ways to equalize funding across school districts—often to a minimum funding level. There are still disparities in funding between wealthy and poorer school districts, but states do recognize the issue and attempt to address it, at least in part.

Revenues are one way to assess education resources. Expenditures are another. Table 5.1 depicts the change in per pupil expenditures since 1969. Note that the dollar figures have been adjusted for inflation according to the consumer price index and are in constant 2013–14 dollars.

Table 5.1   Average per Pupil Expenditures

	U.S. average	Low state	High state
1969–1970	$4,673	$2,841 (Mississippi)	$7,429 (New York)
2011–2012	$11,014	$6,650 (Utah)	$20,492 (District of Columbia)

Source: National Center for Education Statistics (2015).

Even in inflation-adjusted dollars, per pupil expenditures have increased over time. Still, 30 states are providing less funding per student than in 2007, which was the onset of the latest economic downturn. Fourteen states have cut per student funding by more than 10%. Of those states that have increased per student funding, none are located in the south. There is a significant range between states; for example, North Dakota increased per student funding by 31.6% over the past seven years, whereas Oklahoma decreased per student funding by 23.6% (Leachman & Mai, 2014).

What do schools do with this funding? One of the largest expenditures school districts make is providing teachers for students. Again, using constant 2013–14 dollars, Table 5.2 shows how average teacher pay has changed since 1969.

Obviously, the relative "buying power" of teachers' salaries has remained about the same over the past 40 plus years as we look at the change in inflation-adjusted dollars. It is important to consider cost-of-living factors when examining state high and low salaries. For instance, it makes sense that New York would have the highest average salaries while South Dakota has the lowest, given the relative costs of living in those states.

Historically, the promise of a secure and healthy pension has compensated for teachers' relatively low salaries and lack of opportunities for pay raises as compared to other professions. According to the National Council on Teacher Retirement, there are currently $2 trillion being held in trust funds of its member systems (National Council on Teacher Retirements, n.d.). A majority of states still offer a defined benefit plan, which means that educators are guaranteed an amount of annual income after retirement. In

Table 5.2   Average Teacher Salaries

	U.S. average	Low state	High state
1969–1970	$53,655	$36,064 (Mississippi)	$65,685 (Alaska)
2013–2014	$56,689	$40,023 (South Dakota)	$76,566 (New York)

Source: National Center for Education Statistics (2015).

a survey of all state benefit plans, researchers found that annual retirement income "is determined by a formula that takes into account the years of service for the educator in the state and the person's earnings during his or her career" (Toutkoushian, Bathon, & McCarthy, 2011, p. 25). The formulas vary by state and

an educator's gross pension can be affected by a range of factors including the parameters used to calculate a person's first-year pension, whether any caps are placed on the pension, the provisions used for adjusting future pension benefits for cost-of-living increases, and whether the educator can also receive Social Security benefits. Educators also need to take into account the direct costs that they will incur for participating in the state's pension plan. These costs vary from 0% to more than 10% of a person's salary in some states. Similarly, states have different rules for whether pension benefits are subject to state income taxes.

(p. 26)

Defined benefit pension plans are coming under scrutiny due to tighter government budgets and teacher quality reforms. The economic recession starting in 2007–2008 hurt retirement reserves, and long-time underfunding by some states left retirement systems in dire straits. Additionally, defined benefit systems reward teachers for longevity; it usually takes 5 to 10 years to vest in the system, and the retirement benefits increase as one continues to teach. This counteracts some teacher-related reforms like Teach for America, which recruits exceptionally bright college graduates to teach in urban areas. Teach for America only requires a two-year commitment. Therefore, the majority of those teachers, unless they teach beyond their contracted time, will not earn retirement benefits. Other reforms include more rigorous teacher evaluations to allow for easier dismissal of teachers not producing student achievement gains. Policy leaders supporting these and similar reforms see portable defined contribution plans (e.g., 401(k) plans) as more in line with a new teaching workforce.

Finally, a discussion of school finance must acknowledge the role of courts. Since the 1960s, 46 states have been embroiled in some type of school funding litigation (Dinan, 2009). These lawsuits center on the adequacy (not enough funding allocated by the state) and/or equity (funding distributed inequitably across the state) of school funding and have occurred in three phases. Dinan (2009) found that until 1973, litigation generally first took the form of equity suits based in *federal* equal protection claims. This ended in 1973 with the Supreme Court's rejection of a federal equal protection suit (*San Antonio Independent School District v. Rodriguez*). From 1973 to 1988, plaintiffs had only mixed success with equity suits based on *state* equal protection clauses. Recent plaintiffs have had more success with adequacy challenges based on state constitution education clauses (Dinan, 2009).

Since the 1960s, plaintiffs were victorious in 26 states, courts ruled for defendants (the state) in 18 states, and 1 state court offered a mixed opinion (National Access Network, 2014). Fourteen states have current activity regarding school finance litigation, which could include recently filed cases, active trials, or implementation of remedy. Only five states have never had a school finance lawsuit (National Access Network, 2014).

While no state government welcomes litigation or a negative judgment, equity suits generally create more consternation than adequacy suits because equity judgments usually require transferring funds from wealthier districts to poorer districts, while adequacy judgments require an overall increase of funding (Dinan, 2009). Dinan also found that increased state spending as a result of successful school funding litigation does not always translate into increased student achievement outcomes.

These cases have generated an important question for policymakers: What should a quality (or adequate) education cost? For litigation purposes, this is often done through a costing-out study that "determines the amount of money actually needed to make available all of the educational services required to provide every child an opportunity to meet the applicable state education standards" (National Education Access Network, 2006). There are four basic methods states have used. The most popular, used by 14 states, is the professional judgment model. In this approach, "teams of professionals were asked to design an educational program that would meet stated proficiency goals, and to identify all of the specific resources that would be necessary for its success" (National Education Access Network, 2006). Related to this, but less frequently used, is the expert judgment method, which is similar to the professional judgment method, but uses education policy/research experts rather than "in the field" professionals. Nine states have used the successful school district model, which identifies "those school districts that are currently meeting state standards and then [uses] their average expenditure amount as a fair estimate of the actual cost of an adequate education." Finally,

> cost function studies attempt to determine, through analyses of performance measures and cost indices, how much a given school district would need to spend, relative to the average district, to obtain a specific performance target, given the characteristics of the school district and its student body.
>
> (National Education Access Network, 2006)

Major Stakeholders

K–12 education has a plethora of major stakeholders—students, parents, teachers, administrators, support organizations, taxpayers, and policymakers to name a few. Traditionally, teachers' unions have been very influential in federal and state education policy. The two most popular national unions are the National Education Association and the American Federation of Teachers. Both organizations have state-level affiliates. In non-unionized states, teachers still maintain advocacy organizations. Traditionally, these groups have endorsed political candidates and taken stands on proposed legislation. Unions and other educator advocacy organizations have lost some influence over the past decade. Arguably, since the introduction of NCLB legislation, education reforms have focused on student needs, and policymakers have been wary of teachers' conceptions of these needs because unions and other organizations are seen as most interested in the teachers' welfare. This may or may not be a fair impression on the part of policymakers, but it is clear that many policy leaders are turning to groups other than those representing educators to seek input on education reform, including business and civil rights organizations (Cross, 2014).

Another stakeholder group with an increasing amount of influence is foundations. Recent political science research illuminates the impact that foundations are having on education policies. Reckhow and Snyder (2014) found two key reasons why foundations have become so influential in education policy and politics. These include the increase of entities challenging traditional education governance jurisdiction and increased federal activity in education. The jurisdictional challengers are "charter schools and other organizations that compete with or offer alternatives to traditional educational institutions" (Reckhow & Snyder, 2014, p. 190). These challengers may also offer alternatives to traditional teacher certification. The percentage of major foundation grant funding to jurisdictional challengers greatly increased between 2000 and 2010. For example, in 2000, 3% of all education foundation funding went to charter schools, while 16% went to traditional public schools. In 2010, charter school funding was at 16% of the total, but traditional public school grants dropped to 8% (Reckhow & Snyder, 2014). Interestingly, Reckhow and Snyder (2014) also found overlap in agenda and policy goals of major funders. In 2000, 23% of major foundation dollars were given to organizations that had two or more major foundation funders. In 2010, the percentage rose to 64%. Most notable was the alternative teacher preparation program Teach for America, which, in 2010, received money from 13 of the top 15 funders. The Bill and Melinda Gates foundation remains the predominant education foundation in terms of funding (Reckhow & Snyder, 2014).

The increasing federal role in education has also provided an avenue for an increasing role for foundations. Reckhow and Snyder (2014) found that "major education foundations are increasingly politically engaged. . . . Coordinated, policy-focused, and advocacy-oriented philanthropy provides an important pathway for political influence among foundations" (p. 193). For example, Reckhow and Snyder (2014) cite President Obama's inclusion of foundations as part of a group called to work on national education policy issues. Several top foundation staffers have also earned high-level positions at the U.S. Department of Education in recent years. A growing federal presence is consistent with Reckhow and Snyder's (2014) data, which shows the number of national advocacy grantees earning money from the top 15 foundations grew from 7 in 2000 to 34 in 2010, and the total amount of funding for national advocacy and research grew from $56 million to $111 million in the same 10-year time period. The role of foundations in shaping education policy is something to be watched and researched in the years to come.

Major Policy Issues

This chapter will end with a discussion of some recent, impactful policy issues in K–12 education, including charter schools, accountability and accreditation, teacher quality, and college and career readiness. With the number of stakeholders invested in K–12 education and the expectations placed on the public school system by society at large, there are many other policy issues of importance. These four were selected for their timeliness, as debates are ongoing, and their potential impact on K–12 as a whole.

Charter Schools

Charter schools are independently operated public schools authorized (or chartered) by some type of government body (usually a school district or state). Charter schools sprang onto the education policy scene in the early 1990s in Minnesota and now account for 6,440 schools around the nation, or 6% of all public schools (The National Alliance for Public Charter Schools, 2015). The concept behind charter schools is that in exchange for autonomy from some state laws and regulations, the school will meet certain goals. If those goals are not met within a defined period, the school can be closed. The theory is that greater autonomy from bureaucratic rules will allow for innovation that will produce increased student achievement results. What constitutes an "innovation" is widely debated, but charter schools often adopt unique curriculums (e.g., arts-based) or create strong community collaborations for teaching experiences (e.g., a charter school in a museum). Charter schools are also twice as likely as traditional public schools to utilize a year-round school calendar (National Center for Education Statistics, 2014).

Each state can decide whether and how to charter schools. Forty-two states and the District of Columbia allow for charter schools, and these state laws vary by what bodies can authorize schools, how schools are held accountable, and how many schools a state will charter. The freedoms from law and regulation also vary by state, but at a minimum, schools must meet certain federal laws related to civil rights, special education, English language learners, and basic state health and safety rules. Generally, charter schools do not have admissions requirements. If more students want to attend a school than there is space available, a lottery is held. Some claim that charter schools "cream" only the wealthiest or brightest students through targeted marketing, but 54% of charter school students live in poverty, which is greater than the U.S. average (Center for Research on Education Outcomes, 2013). Parents from all corners of society appear to be looking for school choice options. Charter schools can be developed and operated by parents, teachers, community members, or any combination of the above. Charter schools can also be developed by education management organizations (EMOs)—not-for-profit or for-profit entities that operate networks of charter schools.

A good deal of research examines the efficacy and equity of charter schools, and overall, the studies have shown mixed results regarding student academic success, organizational viability, and fiscal responsibility. Still, one of the latest rigorous research studies shows some promising results. The Center for Research on Education Outcomes (CREDO) at Stanford University has conducted many studies on charter schools. Their most recent national study followed up on an earlier study conducted in 2009 which covered charter schools in 27 states that educate 95% of charter school students in the U.S. The 2013 study found that academic achievement improved since 2009. "Charter schools now advance the learning gains of their students more than traditional public schools in reading" (p. 9), with an average of eight additional days of learning (Center for Research on Education Outcomes, 2013). Math learning gains of charter school students were similar to students in traditional public schools. This upward trend in performance corroborates other research out of Vanderbilt University that shows charter school achievement increases over time, once the start-up period is over (Cannata, Thomas, & Thombre, 2014). Charter schools had significant positive impacts on reading and math for students in poverty. When broken down state by state, "the fraction of charter schools that outperform their local [traditional public school] alternatives is 25% of charter schools in reading and 29% in math" (Center for Research on Education Outcomes, 2013, p. 23).

Another CREDO study in 2013 examined EMO and charter management organization (CMO) performance. Although EMOs and CMOs are defined in a variety of ways, the study defines a CMO as a network of three or more charter schools and an EMO as "an organization that provides school operations to independent charter schools and CMOs under contract" (Peltason & Raymond, 2013, p. 3). These can be not-for-profit or for-profit entities. This study investigated 167 CMOs between 2007 and 2011 and found that, on average, these networked schools are "not dramatically better than non-CMO schools in terms of their contributions to student learning" (Peltason & Raymond, 2013, p. 5). The quality varied across the CMOs. Interestingly, "the average student in an EMO school posted significantly more positive learning gains than either CMOs, independent charter schools or the traditional public school comparisons" (Peltason & Raymond, 2013, p. 7). Perhaps the scale and professionalism of EMOs (compared to "mom and pop" charter schools or those that started as an independent school and replicated to a network) contributed to the success of these schools.

State laws on charter schools are expanding. States are removing caps on the number of charter schools, allowing for more autonomy, and increasing accountability. As the movement ages, more is learned about how to make it successful, and charter schools will continue to pose a "dramatic challenge to the education status quo" (Henig, 2013, p. 131).

Accountability and Accreditation

Public school accountability has moved from a sole focus on inputs (e.g., number of books in a library, attendance rates) to a focus on outputs (e.g., student standardized test results, high school graduation rates). This has impacted the way teachers teach, how parents judge schools, and funding models. It has also impacted the long-standing practice of school accreditation. Similar to licensing in early childhood education, accreditation provides a baseline imprimatur of quality. However, parents, the public, and policymakers are now looking at state and federal accountability metrics rather than accreditation to determine the relative quality of a school. Accreditation usually only garners the public's attention when its loss is threatened. Therefore, accrediting agencies must adapt, and AdvancED, the parent organization for the Southern Association of Colleges and Schools, the North Central Association Commission, and the Northwest Accreditation Commission, is a good example of this adaptation. While continuing to perform accreditation functions as it has in one organizational form or another since 1895, it also now acts as a school improvement provider/consultant as schools work toward and beyond accreditation for continuous improvement. AdvancED works with 32,000 schools and school systems in the U.S. and 70 countries. It will be interesting to see whether and how state accountability and school improvement activities coordinate with accreditation activities that essentially overlap each other now.

Teacher Quality

Given the focus on increasing student achievement, it is not surprising that there is a complementary focus on ensuring only quality teachers are in front of the classroom. Some research finds that the top 20% of teachers can generate five to six more months of student learning each year than lower-performing teachers (U.S. Department of Education, 2014b).

There are a couple of strands to this policy focus. One includes accountability, which has been discussed throughout this chapter, and includes evaluating teacher quality based on students' achievement results rather than the traditional method of observations and principal feedback. Another strand is ensuring teacher preparation programs are preparing teachers to be successful in the classroom according to new accountability regimes. There are over 2,000 teacher preparation programs in the U.S., and 90% of them are based at institutions of higher education. Of these 2,000 programs, 69% are traditional (an education degree that then leads to certification), 21% are alternative routes based within institutions of higher education (often abbreviated or fast-track programs), and 10% are alternative routes not located at a university or college (U.S. Department of Education, 2014b). This last category includes Teach for America (TFA), a type of Peace Corps for education where bright college graduates are recruited to teach in urban schools for at least two years and are provided training by TFA.

Over 700,000 people are enrolled in teacher preparation programs, and the vast majority (88%) are in traditional programs. However, while the percentage of future teachers in alternative programs is relatively low, the percentage of program completers is growing much faster at alternative non-college-based programs than at traditional or alternative college-based programs (U.S. Department of Education, 2014b).

Greater emphasis on the efficacy of teacher preparation programs has been building over the past several years. In the 2008 federal Higher Education Act amendments, teacher preparation programs were required to increase reporting requirements (U.S. Department of Education, 2014b). Part of the current evaluation of teacher preparation programs centers on student performance on state licensing or certification exams. Forty-eight states require an assessment for teacher certification, and 41 states use these pass rates for assessment of teacher preparation programs. However, the minimum passing score may be artificially low because the average student score on state exams is 10 to 23 points higher than the minimum score. The pass rates and average scores of test takers did not vary much by the type of preparation program students attended. Under this and other metrics, only 38 teacher preparation programs in 11 states were classified as low-performing or at-risk of low performance in 2011 (U.S. Department of Education, 2014b).

Along with increasing the rigor of teacher preparation programs, the Obama administration is working to ensure all students have access to effective educators. In July 2014, President Obama announced the Excellent Educators for All Initiative. As part of this announcement, Secretary of Education Arne Duncan noted:

> Despite the excellent work and deep commitment of our nation's teachers and principals, systemic inequalities exist that shortchange

students in high-poverty, high-minority schools across our country. We have to do better. Local leaders and educators will develop their own innovative solutions, but we must work together to enhance and invigorate our focus on how to better recruit, support and retain effective teachers and principals for all students, especially the kids who need them most.

(U.S. Department of Education, 2014c)

This pronouncement was followed by guidance to states in November 2014 on designing plans to ensure low-income students have access to highly qualified teachers. States must submit their plans to the federal government in June 2015. Interestingly, these plans do not require student achievement as a measure of teacher quality, which is a departure from previous NCLB waivers issued by the U.S. Department of Education (Klein, 2014).

With all of this policy emphasis on teacher quality potentially indicating that a sizeable percentage of teachers are not of quality now, anecdotes abound about disaffection of teachers. There is no doubt that pressure is increasing on teachers, but recent federal survey data do not show what many might expect. The data points in Table 5.3 were gathered from the 2013 National Center for Education Statistics Schools and Staffing Survey.

Over the past 18 years, teacher satisfaction has remained relatively stable. However, as accountability pressures continue to increase, teacher dissatisfaction and/or shortages may also increase.

Table 5.3   Teacher Satisfaction Statements

Survey statement	% Agree in 1994	% Agree in 2012
"Routine duties and paperwork interfere with my job of teaching."	70.8	69.2
"Level of student misbehavior in this school interferes with my teaching."	44.1	40.7
"I am satisfied with my teaching salary."	44.9	47.0
"I am generally satisfied with being a teacher at this school."	89.7 (2000)	90.2

Source: 2013 National Center for Education Statistics Schools and Staffing Survey.

College and Career Readiness

Given the nation's and states' ambitious educational attainment and economic development goals, more students will need to enter and graduate from college. This means increasing the existing college-going rate of 66% and the college completion rates of 60% or below (depending on type of institution) (National Center for Education Statistics, 2015). Increasing the rigor of high school learning standards is one way to help ensure students are prepared to enter some type of postsecondary education.

Learning standards are not new. Most states have had some type of grade-level and subject matter standards that teachers must teach and students must learn. However, standards varied state to state and were often a mile wide and an inch deep, providing vague direction to teachers and offering little rigor across the board for students. In the mid-2000s, a push began for learning standards benchmarked to college- and career-readiness in an attempt to help build a bridge between high school graduation and a student's next steps. Common rigorous standards across states made sense to many political and educational leaders given the increasingly globally competitive marketplace students would enter upon graduation. Many perceived that students from Michigan would need the same knowledge and skills as students from Alabama. The National Governors Association and the Council of Chief State School Officers collaborated in an unprecedented effort to establish a common core of state standards in reading and math. A number of partners, including Achieve, Inc., College Board, ACT, and university researchers, assisted these two organizations. Developers of the Common Core State Standards (CCSS) examined previous standard-setting efforts and international student comparisons (Conley, 2014). In June 2010, the new "set of clear college- and career-ready standards for kindergarten through 12th grade in English language arts/literacy and mathematics" (Common Core State Standards Initiative, n.d.) were released at an event in a suburb of Atlanta with the Republican governor of Georgia, the Democratic governor of Delaware, chief state school officers, representatives of the NEA and AFT, and educators. This event was clearly meant to be a bipartisan show of support for these standards. Notably, no federal officials were present. Since then, 43 states have adopted the CCSS. Three other states have adopted their own college- and career-ready standards, and two states have adopted most of the CCSS standards, but renamed them something else (Glancy, Fulton, Anderson, Zinth, & Millard, 2014).

According to one academic involved in creating the CCSS, the standards "help educators create *consistency* of expectations, *equity* of opportunity, *clarity* of learning targets, and *economies of scale* as they make decisions about their curriculum and instructional practices" (Conley, 2014). In math, the intent of the standards is to focus on fewer topics, have seamless progression from grade to grade, and promote conceptual understanding. In English language arts/literacy, the goals are to provide students with exposure to complex texts and rigorous vocabulary, build knowledge through content-rich nonfiction, and build reading, writing, and speaking skills (Conley, 2014). Curriculum, related materials, and instructional approaches are left to state and local entities and educators. States can also retain discretion over 15% of their standards and still be considered consistent with the CCSS. Various entities have undertaken studies of the CCSS, and states have compared them to existing state standards as leaders decided whether to adopt them. One group, the conservative-leaning Fordham Institute, stated that the CCSS are "clearer and more rigorous than the vast majority of existing state standards" (Conley, 2014, p. 6).

Although most states have adopted the standards and there was no direct federal involvement in creation of the standards, a backlash of sorts has gained traction fueled by those who believe student learning standards should be a local, rather than national or federal, decision. While not involved in creating the standards, the federal government has certainly praised and encouraged the adoption of CCSS. In order to apply for federal Race to the Top funds, states had to adopt college- and career-ready standards and partake in a common assessment of those standards. The federal government gave hundreds of millions of dollars to consortiums of states to design assessments aligned to the CCSS. The perception of federal involvement was certainly plausible. Now, many legislatures and governors' offices are considering withdrawing from the CCSS and related assessment consortia, and the final outcome is unclear. Pressure remains, however, for states to ensure assessments are rigorous not only in the subject-matter they cover, but also in the "cut-score" used to determine whether the student passes the assessment. The National Assessment of Educational Progress (NAEP) is administered through the U.S. Department of Education to a sample of U.S. students every other year or so (depending on grade and subject). NAEP deems a student "proficient" if the student has "demonstrated competency over challenging subject matter, including subject-matter knowledge, application of such knowledge to real-world situations, and analytical skills approximate to the subject matter" (Achieve, Inc., 2015, p. 1). In analyzing student proficiency rates on state standardized tests as compared to what students in that state had achieved on the NAEP tests, large discrepancies were found. Over half of states have student proficiency rates on state standardized tests 30 percentage points higher than what students in that state achieved on the nationally normed NAEP tests (Achieve, Inc., 2015). The silver lining in this rather gloomy report that characterizes states as not really expecting much of students is that many states have committed to implementing new assessments in alignment with college- and career-ready standards. Those should be implemented in the next couple of years.

Some potential advantages to a common set of college- and career-ready standards and related assessments across states include:

- Greater collaboration between states to share best practices and find cost-sharing efficiencies
- Higher levels of learning for students
- The ability to compare achievement across states as students will be learning the same material and will be assessed in similar ways
- Building a bridge between early learning programs and kindergarten because what a kindergartener must know will be clearly spelled out
- Equality of opportunity for all students no matter where they live or whether they are highly mobile.

Some potential costs to implementation of common college- and career-ready standards include:

- The need to redesign teacher preparation programs to ensure teachers are aware of the new standards and how to teach them
- Lack of local and state control of standards

● The possibility that the subject-matter rigor in early grades reduces time for focus on other developmental skills.

The development of common standards has also generated discussion on what "college- and career-ready" really means. Do students wishing to enter college or follow a certain career path after high school require the same high school curriculum? Most policymakers and education advocacy groups are saying yes. Achieve, Inc. (2012) offers definitions that seem to be widely shared among policymakers across the nation. College-ready means

> being prepared for any postsecondary experience, including study at two- and four-year institutions leading to a postsecondary credential (i.e. a certificate, license, Associate's or Bachelor's degree). Being academically ready for college means that a high school graduate has the English and mathematics knowledge and skills necessary to qualify for and succeed in entry-level, credit-bearing college coursework without the need for remedial coursework.

A career-ready student "has the English and math knowledge and skills needed to qualify for and succeed in the postsecondary job training and/or education necessary for their chosen career (i.e. technical/vocational program, community college, apprenticeship or significant on-the-job training)." Both definitions consider that high school graduates will need some postsecondary training. Interestingly, though, funding cuts and increased emphasis on college for all have lessened emphasis on career counseling in America's high schools. So, high schools may be ensuring students are career-ready without ensuring students know for what career.

Looking Forward

From who governs schools, to how schools are funded, to what schools must teach, performance is key. All of the debates described in this chapter detail conflicting views on what will improve K–12 education. In the last decade or so, improvement and accountability have focused on standardized test scores, and policy debates have focused on levers to increase that performance. Policy leaders have tinkered with governance structures, funding models, and accountability regimes all in the name of increasing student performance. No one policy or combination of policies has yet to cause consistently increasing achievement in all settings for all students. Recently released research found that the vast amount of federal funds sent to states and local school districts to improve the lowest-performing schools are not very effective, as only one-third of schools receiving federal School Improvement Grants improved over time (Layton, 2015).

State K–12 chiefs continue to turn over at fast rates, and governors wrestle with them and legislatures for control over education policy. Education reform movements such as charter schools and teacher accountability practices are coming of age, and increasing data and more sophisticated practices will allow policymakers see if they are meeting their aims. Meanwhile, the federal government continues to debate the reauthorization of its landmark education bill, which could have major implications for state and local programs of education.

As of May 2015, Congress is actively working on the reauthorization of ESEA. The House of Representatives has considered a reauthorization bill, largely backed by House Republicans, entitled the "Student Success Act," but discussion has been tabled (Camera, 2015a). The Senate education committee drafted a bipartisan rewrite of NCLB that passed committee in April 2015 by a vote of 22–0 (Camera, 2015b). It has not yet been taken up by the full Senate. When and if the House and Senate approve a bill reauthorizing the ESEA, they will need to negotiate with each other and the White House on specific provisions of the bill. Major themes being debated in both chambers include whether to make any changes to ESEA's current requirement for annual state testing of students and whether to allow flexibility in state and local school district allocation of Title I funds. One observer of Washington, DC, politics notes:

> The bottom line is that we cannot seem to agree on a national education policy. We can't settle on what standards to put in place and whether they should be national or state-by-state. We can't decide what range of school choice to allow, what amount of testing makes sense, how to ensure teacher quality and what levels of funding are necessary. We are even further from any meaningful consensus on who should have ultimate control.
>
> (Harkness, 2015, p. 16)

It will be interesting to follow whether meaningful traction is made in reauthorizing ESEA or whether the bill is caught up, as many others are, in what seem to be increasingly partisan politics.

For Further Information

- Education Commission of the States is a national organization that provides policy information to states on early learning through higher education topics: www.ecs.org
- *Education Week* is a weekly newspaper focused on K–12 topics: www.edweek.org
- The U.S. Department of Education website provides information about all federal government-administered education programs: www.ed.gov
- The Center for Education Policy is a Washington, DC, based independent think tank on K–12 education: www.cep-dc.org/
- RealClearEducation is a free daily news service on early childhood through higher education issues: http://realcleareducation.com/
- *Education Next*, sponsored by Stanford University's Hoover Institution, the Fordham Institute, and Harvard's Kennedy School Program on Education Policy and Governance, is a cross between a research journal and policy magazine: http://educationnext.org/
- The Hechinger Report provides in-depth education reporting: http://hechingerreport.org/

Note

1. There are some exceptions at the front and tail ends of this grade span. Some states do not require kindergarten, and some states allow teenagers to drop out of high school upon reaching a certain age, usually 17 or 18 years old.

References

Achieve, Inc. (2012). *What does college- and career-ready really mean?* Retrieved from www.achieve.org/what-college-and-career-ready
Achieve, Inc. (2015). *Proficient vs. prepared: Disparities between state tests and the 2013 National Assessment of Educational Progress (NAEP).* Retrieved from www.achieve.org/naepbrief

Camera, L. (2015a, March 4). House wrestles with NCLB rewrite bill. *Education Week.*

Camera, L. (2015b, April 16). Senate education committee unanimously passes bipartisan ESEA rewrite. *Education Week.*

Cannata, M., Thomas, G., & Thombre, Z. (2014). *Starting strong: Best practices in starting a charter school.* Nashville, TN: Vanderbilt Peabody College.

Center for Research on Education Outcomes. (2013). *National charter school study executive summary.* Retrieved from http://credo.stanford.edu

Common Core State Standards Initiative. (n.d.). *Frequently asked questions.* Retrieved from www.corestandards.org/about-the-standards/frequently-asked-questions/

Conley, D. (2014). Common Core: Development and substance. *Social Policy Report, 28*(2). Retrieved from www.srcd.org/sites/default/files/spr282_final.pdf

Cross, C. (2014). *Political education: Setting the course for state and federal policy* (2nd ed.) New York, NY: Teachers College Press.

Dinan, J. (2009). School finance litigation: the third wave recedes. In J. Dunn and M. West (Eds.), From schoolhouse to courthouse: the judiciary's role in American education (pp. 96–120). Washington, D.C.: Brookings Institution Press.

Education Commission of the States. (2014). *Governance: State boards/chiefs/agencies.* Retrieved from www.ecs.org/html/issue.asp?issueid=68&subIssueID=217

Education Commission of the States. (2015). *Local school boards—50 state analysis.* Retrieved from http://ecs.force.com/mbdata/mbquestU?SID=a0i70000006ev YW&rep=K12G713&Q=Q0646

Education Week Research Center. (2014a). *Chance for success metrics.* Retrieved from www.edweek.org/media/16qc-chanceforsuccess-c1.pdf

Education Week Research Center. (2014b). *Views of a changing landscape.* Retrieved from www.edweek.org/ew/qc/2014/complex-school-district-environment.html? r=1113010295&preview=1

Glancy, E., Fulton, M., Anderson, L., Zinth, J., & Millard, M. (2014, October). *Blueprint for college readiness: A 50-state policy analysis.* Retrieved from www.ecs. org/docs/BlueprintforCollegeReadiness.pdf

GradNation. (2015, May 12). *Building a grad nation: Progress and challenge in ending the high school dropout epidemic: Executive summary.* Retrieved from http://gradnation. org/report/2015-building-grad-nation-report

Harkness, P. (2015, May). Washington's education stalemate. *Governing*, pp.16–17.

Henig, J. (2013). *The end of exceptionalism in American education.* Cambridge, MA: Harvard Education Press.

Klein, A. (2014, November 10). Ed. Dept. directs states to improve teacher distribution. *Education Week.*

Kline, J. (2014, November 13). *Kline statement on Education Department's new waiver guidance.* Retrieved from http://edworkforce.house.gov/news/documentsingle. aspx?DocumentID=398168

Layton, L. (2015, May 5). "Most states lacked expertise to improve worst schools." The Washington Post. Retrieved from: www.washingtonpost.com/local/edu cation/most-states-lacked-expertise-to-improve-worst-schools/2015/05/05/0eb82b98-f35f-11e4-bcc4-e8141e5eb0c9_story.html

Leachman, M., & Mai, C. (2014, October 16). *Most states still funding schools less than before the recession.* Retrieved from www.cbpp.org/research/most-states-still-funding-schools-less-than-before-the-recession

McAdams, D. (2006). *What school boards can do: Reform governance for urban schools.* New York, NY: Teachers College Press.

National Access Network. (2014, May). *Litigations challenging constitutionality of K–12 funding in the 50 states.* Retrieved from http://schoolfunding.info/wp-content/uploads/2014/05/Litigations-Challenging-Constitutionality-of-K-12-Funding.pdf

The National Alliance for Public Charter Schools. (2015). *The public charter schools dashboard.* Retrieved from http://dashboard.publiccharters.org/dashboard/schools/year/2014

National Center for Education Statistics. (2014). *Digest of education statistics.* Retrieved from www.nces.ed.gov

National Center for Education Statistics. (2015). *Digest of education statistics.* Retrieved from www.nces.ed.gov

National Council on Teacher Retirements. (n.d.). *NCTR by the numbers.* Retrieved from www.nctr.org/about-nctr/

National Education Access Network. (2006). *A costing out primer.* Retrieved from http://schoolfunding.info/policy-research/costing-out-studies-2/a-costing-out-primer/

Peltason, E., & Raymond, M. (2013, January 30). *Charter school growth and replication Vol. I.* Retrieved from the http://credo.stanford.edu/pdfs/CGAR%20Growth%20Volume%20I.pdf

Reckhow, S., & Snyder, J. (2014). The expanding role of philanthropy in education politics. *Educational Researcher, 43*(4), 186–195.

Roza, M. (2013). How current education governance distorts financial decision-making. In P. Manna & P. McGuinn (Eds.), *Education governance for the twenty-first century* (pp. 36–57). Washington, DC: Brookings Institute Press.

Scudella, V. (2013). *State education governance models.* Retrieved from www.ecs.org/clearinghouse/01/08/70/10870.pdf

Shober, A. (2012). Governors make the grade: Growing gubernatorial influence in state education policy. *Peabody Journal of Education, 87*(5), 559–575.

Toutkoushian, R., Bathon, J., & McCarthy, M. (2011). A national study of the net benefits of state pension plans for educators. *Journal of Education Finance, 37*(1), 24–51.

Ujifusa, A. (2014, January 9). State, local officials square off on who calls shots on K–12. *Education Week.*

U.S. Department of Education. (2012, June 7). *ESEA flexibility.* Retrieved from www2.ed.gov/policy/elsec/guid/esea-flexibility/index.html

U.S. Department of Education (2014a). *Fact sheet: Elementary and Secondary Act flexibility.* Retrieved from www.ed.gov/news/press-releases/fact-sheet-elementary-and-secondary-education-act-flexibility

U.S. Department of Education (2014b). *Improving teacher preparation: Building on innovation.* Retrieved from www.ed.gov/teacherprep

U.S. Department of Education. (2014c). *New initiative to provide all students access to great educators.* Retrieved from www.ed.gov/news/press-releases/new-initiative-provide-all-students-access-great-educators

Chapter 6

Higher Education

Introduction

Higher education[1] is a complex field characterized by dramatic growth over the last several decades, various types of public and private institutions, a tradition of autonomy, and numerous expectations. It is no longer a system just for the elite or the wealthy; it is theoretically open to all who are interested and qualified. This does not mean there is equal access yet, as evidenced by the various statistics about who enrolls in higher education and completes a degree. Yet, more people than ever are attending. Reflecting this dichotomy is a recent survey which found that 55% of respondents (in a random sample of about 1,000 people) believe college is necessary for a person to be successful in today's workforce, up from 31% of respondents in 2000. However, only 29% of respondents believe that the vast majority of people who are qualified to go to college have the opportunity to do so, down from 45% in 2000 (Immerwahr & Johnson, 2009). Although there are myriad policy issues surrounding higher education, including access to college, many believe that the American system of higher education "remains the envy of the world" (Birnbaum, 1988, p. 3). This chapter will outline the governance and finance structures of today's higher education landscape as well as present some salient policy issues. The complexity of the field cannot be understated—increasing numbers and diversity of students and decreasing financial support are coupled with calls for greater institutional and system efficiency and effectiveness. This chapter attempts to shed light on these trends and help the reader navigate the complexity.

Given the variety of institutions and the great change over time in the field of higher education, it is important to provide some initial context with the current landscape of institutions, students, and faculty.

Institutions

There are 4,724 institutions of higher education in the United States. About 3,000 of these are four-year institutions and 1,700 are two-year institutions. The majority of institutions (3,099) are privately controlled and 1,625 are public institutions (National Center for Education Statistics, 2015). The degree-granting status of the institution and whether it is publicly or privately controlled are just two of several institutional variations. A privately controlled institution can be not-for-profit, such as Harvard University, or for-profit, such as the University of Phoenix. An institution can be research intensive, with an emphasis on external grant funding, graduate education, and faculty publications, or it can be open access, with a focus on helping marginally prepared students successfully complete a college degree. A college can focus on liberal arts or career and technical education. It can be in the middle of an urban city or in the idyllic countryside. Some institutions now have 100,000 or more students, whereas others enroll just a thousand or so students. Interestingly, the institution of higher education with the greatest number of enrolled students is the University of Phoenix with over 200,000 students, down from its peak of 475,000 students in 2010 (Fain, 2015).

The selectivity of institutions varies by sector. The overwhelming majority (87%) of four-year colleges admit 50% or more of their applicants, and 90% of two-year institutions have no admissions criteria. Almost 75% of private, for-profit institutions (two- and four-year) have no admissions criteria, while only 18% of public, four-year institutions are open access (National Center for Education Statistics, 2015). One policy issue surrounding selectivity is which students are accepted where. For example, are low-income or racial minorities underrepresented at elite institutions and overrepresented at open access institutions? This matters because elite institutions boast higher completion rates and greater perceived employment prospects (e.g., jobs and salaries). Data provided throughout this chapter will shed some light on this question, but it is an area worthy of in-depth study.

Overall, in 2014, Harvard University accepted just 5.9% of 35,000 applicants. Stanford University accepted 5.07% of its applicants. Other top-tier schools were not as selective. For example, the University of Michigan accepted 32% of its applicants and Notre Dame accepted 21%. What these rates do not show is the percentage of the applicant pool qualified for admittance to these schools. Although from year to year it seems that admission rates are shrinking, it isn't because of greater numbers of students applying to selective schools or fewer spots at these schools. Rather, the seemingly shrinking admissions rates are causing more students to apply to more schools, so the pool of applicants at each school is growing. It is estimated that 80% of top students get into at least one top school (Carey, 2014).

Students

Almost 40% of working adults aged 25 to 64 have a two- or four-year postsecondary degree ("Quality Counts Report," 2014). Greater numbers and percentages of students than ever before are matriculating from high school to college. In 1960, only 45% of high school graduates enrolled in college within 12 months. Today, 66% of high school graduates enroll in college (National Center for Education Statistics, 2015), ranking the U.S. in ninth place among economically similar countries (OECD, 2014). The data also show that females enter college at a higher rate than males, although the most recent data show that the gap is closing somewhat. Students from wealthy families enter at a rate 30 percentage points higher than high school graduates from low-income families. Race also plays a role in whether a high school completer attends college; 81% of Asian high school graduates enroll in college compared to 67% of White students, 57% of Black students, and 66% of Hispanic students (National Center for Education Statistics, 2015). Although disparities are evident, rates for all groups are increasing over time. It is important to recognize that these figures only count students who made it to high school graduation and not the entire age cohort.

In looking at the full age cohort, in 1967, only 25.5% of 18- to 24-year-olds were enrolled in degree-granting institutions. By 2013, the rate was at 40% (National Center for Education Statistics, 2015). As of fall 2013, 14.9 million students were enrolled at public degree-granting institutions, and 5.7 million were enrolled at private institutions (National Center for Education Statistics, 2015).

Hopefully, postsecondary enrollment leads to degree attainment. The number of degrees has increased over time, as has the percentage of degrees earned by women. In 1920, over 48,000 bachelor's degrees were awarded (34% to women), over 4,000 master's degrees were awarded (30% to women), and 615 doctoral degrees were awarded (15% to women). In 2011–12, 1.8 million bachelor's degrees were awarded (57% to women), 754,000 master's degrees were awarded (60% to women), and 170,000 doctoral degrees were awarded (51% to women). In addition, slightly over 1 million associate's degrees were awarded in 2011–12 (National Center for Education Statistics, 2015).

As noted earlier, higher education is comprised of various types of institutions. Table 6.1 depicts the percentage of students enrolled at each type of institution by enrollment status.

Table 6.1   Student Enrollment Patterns (2012)

	% of all students enrolled in sector	In the sector, the percentage of students who are:		
		Full-time undergraduate	Part-time undergraduate	All graduate
Public two-year	33%	38%	61%	n/a
Public four-year	38%	63%	19%	17%
Private non-profit four-year	19%	57%	12%	31%
For-profit	10%	50%	19%	14%
Total	100%	—	—	—

Source: Data from College Board (2014a).

Faculty

Today, there are 1.5 million faculty members among the variety of higher education institutions. Slightly more than 50% of these faculty members are full-time employees and slightly less than 50% are female. Of the 1.5 million faculty, 968,000 (64%) are in public institutions, 449,000 (30%) are in private nonprofit institutions, and 128,000 (9%) are in private for-profit institutions. Over 1.1 million faculty members work in four-year institutions while under 400,000 are in two-year institutions (National Center for Education Statistics, 2015).

Although there are wide variations in salary by what type of institution the faculty member works at (e.g., faculty at research universities tend to earn more) and by the rank of the individual professor (e.g., full professors tend to earn more than assistant professors or lecturers), it is notable that faculty average salaries have not made dramatic gains over the past 40 years. In 2012–13, full-time faculty members on nine-month contracts (no summer teaching), on average, earned $77,301, up slightly from $69,494 in 1975–76 (in constant 2012–13 dollars). Breaking this number down by control of the institution (public versus private) shows that faculty salaries at public institutions moved only slightly, whereas salaries at private institutions saw a $20,000 leap over the past 40 years (National Center for Education Statistics, 2015).

Some higher education faculty have the opportunity to earn tenure. According to the American Association of University Professors[2], "tenure, briefly stated, is an arrangement whereby faculty members, after successful completion of a period of probationary service, can be dismissed only for adequate cause or other possible circumstances and only after a hearing before a faculty committee." Traditionally, tenure helps to preserve academic freedom—the ability of a faculty member to conduct research in the pursuit of truth, absent any political or other interference. At public four-year institutions with a tenure system, 65% of full-time faculty have tenure. This is down from 70% in 1993–94. For private nonprofit institutions, 44% of full-time faculty have tenure, down from 50% in 1993–94 (College Board, 2014a).

Governance

The variety of higher education institutions necessitates a variety of governance structures at state and institutional levels. Although the federal government does not necessarily govern higher education given states' constitutional authority over education, it still exercises a substantial amount of influence. An eminent higher education scholar defines governance as "the structures and processes through which institutional participants interact with and influence each other and communicate with the larger environment" (Birnbaum, 1988, p. 4). There are several ways in which the governance structures of higher education institutions differ from other organizations (Birnbaum, 1988). First, rather than a mixture of professional and nonprofessional employees, the organization is primarily composed of highly educated professionals both at the faculty and administrative levels. Sometimes faculty do not always identify themselves with the institution, but rather they feel more loyalty to their fields (e.g., biology, political science) and colleagues in that field around the country and world. While the two previous differences are more likely to occur at research-focused higher education institutions, the next two differences occur at all types of institutions. Faculty are most often organized into colleges (e.g., the college of education) and departments (e.g., the educational leadership department). The colleges and departments have their own hierarchies and goals and priorities, and this leads to a governance structure of nesting subunits. Again, rather than allegiance to the larger organization, faculty typically collaborate with faculty in their department or college, and important personnel decisions (hiring, promotions, salaries) are often handled at that level as well. Finally, institutions of higher education are saddled with many important, but sometimes conflicting, goals (Birnbaum, 1988). For instance, institutions are expected to increase access to college while maintaining or increasing the quality of instruction and outcomes.

Even with these governance issues, something is still going well, as U.S. institutions of higher education are generally respected around the world. Several U.S. research universities appear in any type of worldwide institutional rankings. So, as Birnbaum (1988) questions, how can American institutions of higher education be both poorly run (in his opinion) and highly effective? The answer lies in the institutions' complexity.

Federal

Similar to early learning and K–12 education, the federal government exerts influence over higher education through a variety of means. Given lack of direct authority per the U.S. Constitution, there are two primary ways that the federal government influences higher education: providing funding for students and research and "setting, interpreting, and enforcing civil rights legislation that affects colleges and universities" (Gladieux, King, & Corrigan, 2005, p. 163). In fact, the federal government's expenditures on student aid and research outpace state expenditures in those areas (Gladieux et al., 2005).

There are several exhaustive and detailed histories of higher education that outline the federal government's involvement with colleges and universities throughout the history of the United States. This section will highlight just a couple of key periods and initiatives to provide context for the federal government's involvement in higher education policy today.

Arguably, the first significant federal higher education initiative was the passage of the Morrill Land-Grant College Act of 1862. This act provided states grants of land to establish colleges that focused on practical arts such as agriculture, engineering, and home economics. Initiated by Congressman Morrill from Vermont and signed by President Lincoln, the purported reasons for the legislation included "democratization of higher education; the development of an educational system deliberately planned to meet utilitarian ends through research and public service as well as instruction; and a desire to emphasize the emerging applied sciences, particularly agricultural science and engineering" (Williams, 1991, p. 1). The act did not instigate land-grant colleges' immediate success, as it only provided for grants of land, not operating funds. Between 1862 and 1887, all 37 states at the time established a land-grant college or planned to do so, but enrollments were small and the organizations were tenuous. Two subsequent federal acts bolstered these colleges. The Hatch Act of 1887 provided funding for agricultural experiment stations that were attached to the land-grant colleges, and the 1890 Morrill Act provided the needed annual federal funding for general academic programs at the land-grant colleges (Williams, 1991). Many of these original land-grant colleges retain their land-grant missions and are the flagship institutions of their respective states, including the University of California, the University of Florida, and the Massachusetts Institute of Technology. These institutions are some of the largest and highest ranked public colleges in the U.S. and the world that simultaneously provide services to their state.

The period after World War II was one of great expansion and diversity for higher education, and it happened somewhat by accident. The Serviceman's Readjustment Act of 1944 (commonly known as the GI Bill) was developed as the federal government considered how to successfully integrate returning veterans into the new the post-war economy (Thelin, 2004). The act gave veterans college tuition assistance and living expenses. Government leaders' projections of how many veterans would utilize this benefit were very low. However, "by 1950, of the fourteen million eligible veterans, more than two million, or 16 percent, had opted to enroll in postsecondary education" (Thelin, 2004, p. 363). Women veterans enrolled at a higher rate than male veterans (30% versus 18%). Results of this major expansion included significant growth, sometimes doubling, of college enrollments; increased federal reliance, and hence growth, of accrediting agencies to certify institutions eligible to receive GI benefits; and increasing use of standardized tests for admissions purposes as colleges struggled to sort through the deluge of applicants (Thelin, 2004). The growth of the higher education sector did not happen solely on idyllic, moss-strewn, four-year colleges. The transition to mass higher education led to the growth of new institutional forms such as community colleges and trade schools. "One estimate was that on the average, a new public community campus opened each week during the decade starting in 1960" (Thelin, 2004, p. 300). The GI Bill's impact can be seen in the growth of the total number of students enrolled in postsecondary education over the years. In 1939, a little less than 1.5 million students were enrolled in college. In 1949 this grew to 2.7 million, and by 1970, 7.9 million were enrolled (Thelin, 2004).

Also after World War II, President Truman established a commission on higher education in 1946 to examine "the functions of higher education in our democracy and the means by which they can best be performed" (Thelin, 2004, p. 268, quoting the commission report). This was the first time a U.S. president "deliberately extended federal inquiry into nationwide educational issues" (Thelin, 2004, p. 268). The commission produced many far-reaching proposals, many of which were not adopted by President Truman but were adopted by succeeding presidential administrations. These included increased governmental support for higher education, the need for greater racial integration and diversity within higher education, and more attention to community colleges as access points into America's higher education system (Thelin, 2004).

In 1965, President Johnson extended the federal government's reach into higher education with the passage of the Higher Education Act (HEA). Among other things, this act provided research grants to institutions, need-based aid for students, and support for teacher preparation at institutions of higher education (Thelin, 2004). The 1972 HEA amendments were significant given the inclusion of Title IX, which "prohibited discrimination based on sex in any educational program" that received federal support and/or funding. Although Title IX covers all instances of gender discrimination, it is primarily associated with athletics, as that is where the greatest instances of gender discrimination occurred (Thelin, 2004). The 1998 HEA amendments included an emphasis on preparation for college and initiated the GEAR UP program (Gaining Early Awareness and Readiness for Undergraduate Programs) (Thelin, 2004). Grants are awarded to states and partnerships to provide services to high poverty middle and high schools. In fact, activities must start no later than with seventh grade cohorts. In fiscal year 2014, 128 GEAR UP awards were made, totaling over $300 million dollars and serving over half a million students.

The HEA was due for reauthorization in 2014 and it is still pending. The Senate Committee on Health, Education, Labor, and Pensions made significant movement toward reauthorization in the spring of 2015, particularly through leadership of its chair Senator Lamar Alexander (R-TN). The committee's focus for reauthorization is improving quality and innovation through removing unnecessary and burdensome regulations on institutions of higher education (Stratford, 2015a). A bipartisan segment of the committee commissioned a report on federal higher education regulations from 16 higher education leaders and the American Council on Education. One of the committee co-chairs, Nicholas Zeppos, president of Vanderbilt University, stated at a committee hearing "that an internal study of his institution showed that federal red tape relating to higher education cost the university $14 million annually" (Stratford, 2015a).

These described federal initiatives laid the foundation for future presidential endeavors into higher education policy. The remainder of this section will touch on a few highlights of President Obama's higher education policy agenda. Arguably undergirding all other initiatives is the president's focus on college completion and attainment. Until recently, average four-year graduation rates of 50% (and lower for some groups of students) were the norm. Success in higher education was—and is to a certain extent still—seen as the responsibility of the student. The vast majority of college students are 18 years or older, and many are living apart from parents and guardians for the first time. In the eyes of the law, at least, they are adults. Times have changed, and society seems to be recognizing that adolescence lasts beyond attainment of legal adulthood. Couple this with an economic imperative to increase national and state education attainment rates, and more pressure is placed on institutions of higher education to help students succeed. In President Obama's first address to a joint session of Congress in 2009, he set a goal for the U.S. to lead the world in college completion by 2020 (Field, 2015). The U.S. had once lead the world in this metric, but other countries had quickly caught up and surpassed the nation's rate for percentage of adults with some postsecondary credential. The president's goal means that the U.S. would need to increase its educational attainment rate from 39% to 56%, requiring an additional 8 million associate's and bachelor's degrees. This assumes all other competing countries' rates will remain static, which will certainly not happen because South Korea, which is ranked higher than the U.S., has already increased its rate. As of 2015, five years until the goal deadline, the U.S. had only increased its national ranking by one place to 11th overall. Regardless of the ranking, the attainment rate did increase from 39% to 44% over six years, which is not a small feat. Other successes include 10% more students enrolled at four-year colleges than in 2009 and a 15% increase in the number of degrees conferred (Field, 2015). While the goal to increase educational attainment is laudable for both economic and individual growth reasons, some may ask whether international rankings are important given the inability to rely on the proffered data. For instance, some countries' populations are decreasing each year (low birth rates), which gives them an advantage in calculating the percentage of citizens with a degree (Hauptman, 2013). Further, some countries factor vocational certificates into their count, but the U.S. does not. Whether or not being number one in the world is important, it does seem to make sense for colleges to help those who enroll to succeed rather than passively to monitor matriculation. Many major foundations and organizations, such as the Lumina Foundation, the Bill and Melinda Gates Foundation, Complete College America, and the National Governors Association, agree with President Obama and have devoted significant amounts of money and other support for states and higher education institutions to develop policy and programs geared toward increasing completion and attainment.

College completion rates are anticipated to be part of President Obama's college rating initiative. Public transparency of institutional information was a recommendation of U.S. Secretary of Education Margaret Spellings's 2006 commission on the future of higher education. Transparency and accountability at all levels of education, including higher education, have, to a great extent, become bipartisan issues, so even though Secretary Spellings served under Republican President George W. Bush, President Obama continued and furthered this policy. The goals of President Obama's current ratings plan go beyond consumer transparency and tie financial support to college performance on a defined set of metrics; challenge states to fund institutions based on performance; and hold students and colleges accountable for making progress toward a degree (Mangan & Supiano, 2014). A draft of the ratings system was released in December 2014, and the proposed metrics included:

- The percentage of students receiving Pell grants as a measure of access
- Enrolled students' average "expected family contribution" or the amount the federal government deems a family can pay for college
- Family income quintiles to show the socioeconomic diversity of the college
- The percentage of students who are first-generation college-goers
- The average net price students pay after grants and scholarships are applied to tuition
- The average net price by income quintile, which provides potential students with information on what students in their income bracket might pay
- College completion rates

- Student transfer rates from community colleges to four-year institutions (if applicable)
- Labor market success of students
- Graduate school attendance of completing students
- Loan performance outcomes such as deferment, forbearance, and repayment rates (Mangan & Supiano, 2014).

Although eventually expected, relative weighting was not yet assigned to the metrics, and there was no indication yet as to how similar institutions will be grouped. The first ratings are scheduled to be released in the fall of 2015. There is much consternation about the rating system, particularly about how to provide accurate, relevant, and comparable information on institutions that are so diverse. The president of the Association of Private Sector Colleges and Universities likely summed up many stakeholders' beliefs, noting that the extensive amount of time it took the U.S. Department of Education to come up with the initial draft of the ratings "seems to support the long-held belief by many in higher education that while a college-rating system is admirable in theory, it is not feasible to create metrics that definitively assess the quality of so many institutions across the country" (Field, 2014). Even without the rankings, there remain several avenues of web-based transparency, including two federal initiatives: the College Navigator, which is intended to help students pick a college, and the College Scorecard, which provides information on costs of college, graduation rates, student loans, and employment statistics.

State

Responsibility for the provision of higher education rests with the states. Until about 50 years ago, states offered minimal oversight and coordination of public institutions. Since then, states have increasingly organized their public institutions of higher education into systems (Johnstone, 2013). Some states have one system for all institutions, while others divide technical, two-year, four-year, and research institutions into two or more systems. Systems are generally structured as governing or coordinating agencies. A couple of states utilize planning agencies, which have virtually no authority over institutions, but rather collect and disseminate information about higher education to state leaders (McGuinness, 2005). Governing boards centralize authority over state public higher education institutions into a state-level corporate body, whereas coordinating boards "merely provide an interface between the state government and the governing boards of the state's systems and individual colleges and universities" (Nicholson-Crotty & Meier, 2004, p. 85). Governing boards also have more autonomy from other state actors than coordinating boards (Nicholson-Crotty & Meier, 2004) and assume greater operational authority over institutions, including hiring the institution's president (Hendrickson, Lane, Harris, & Dorman, 2013). Seventeen states utilize governing systems and 31 have coordinating agencies. In 42 states, the governor appoints the majority of higher education agency board members (Education Commission of the States, 2014). The previous paragraph provides some "bright-line" ways to categorize state higher education governance systems, but it is important to note that the governance structures of any two states are not exactly the same (McLendon & Ness, 2003) because state history, culture, politics, and policies contexts vary considerably. The type of higher education structure employed by the state has been shown to affect higher education policies. For example, Knott and Payne (2004) found that states with the highest state regulation of institutions had the lowest tuition rates, research funding, and productivity (as measured by the number of faculty-published articles).

State system leadership is a difficult job. As the following quote notes, governing boards (and arguably sometimes coordinating boards) must be the bridges between state leaders and higher education institutions and work to balance both sets of interests:

> As an agent of the state—whether appointed or elected—the governing board represents the interests of the public, including the efficient use of tax revenues, the need for the university to attend to the needs of commerce and the larger economy, and the role of colleges and universities in promoting social and political goals such as equity and diversity. . . . At the same time, the governing board needs to advocate on behalf of the institution or system to the state government, especially for resources, with the political leverage that the board is presumed to have

via its gubernatorial appointment and legislative approval or its direct election, as well as to shield the university from the political or popular slings and arrows that are often sent in the direction of the academy.

(Johnstone, 2013, p. 79)

Perhaps this is why turnover of state system leaders is so high. As of 2013, almost half of state system leaders had been in their positions for two years or less (McGuinness, 2013).

Beyond state and/or institutional board appointment powers, governors can influence higher education through the budgeting process and creation of policy initiatives. Governors often choose to highlight important policy initiatives in annual state of the state addresses. In an analysis of 48 gubernatorial state-of-the-state speeches from 2015, 27 governors highlighted the role of higher education regarding workforce development, 23 governors focused on postsecondary funding and affordability, 11 governors either praised dual enrollment programs or called for greater alignment between K–12 and higher education, and 6 governors specifically called for higher state postsecondary educational attainment rates (American Association of State Colleges and Universities, 2015). Higher education is certainly a prominent agenda item for current state governors.

As with all policy areas, state legislatures hold ultimate authority in voting something into law (unless the governor wields a veto that is not overturned). This is true of higher education policy as well. Governors, state agencies, and legislatures often consider whether a policy initiative can be just that—an initiative—or must be written into law. For example, state college completion policies are sometimes initiatives of the state higher education agency and/or the governor, and sometimes they are initiatives of the legislature and are written into law (e.g., college president evaluations being based on college completion rates could be an agency initiative or law). Often, collaboration between all stakeholders and leaders helps decide what policies need to be administered, regulated, or legislated.

It is also important to note the role of private higher education institutions within state systems. The limits to state interference in private college governance were settled long ago by the U.S. Supreme Court in *Trustees of Dartmouth College v. Woodward* (1819), when the court ruled that the New

Hampshire state legislature could not unilaterally amend the college's corporate charter. Still, although they are not part of the public system and are protected by law as private corporations, states provide some regulation for private institutions, in part to protect citizens and employers from institutions that take student money but provide little value in return (e.g., diploma mills). Some states even provide public funds to private institutions, recognizing them as an important part of the state higher education ecosystem. In 2010,

> 14 states provided more than $200 billion to their private colleges and universities. With the exception of Louisiana, all these states are east of the Mississippi River, and state support of private higher education in these states is likely because of the strength of the private sectors there.
> (Hendrickson et al., 2013, p. 129)

Institutional

Unlike early learning and K–12 education, it is important to discuss institutional-level governance in the context of American higher education because institutions maintain a good amount of autonomy. Depending on the state higher education governance structure, public institutions may have an institutional-level governing board, an advisory board, or no board at all. Private institutions utilize some type of institutional board to govern the organization and oversee the president. A survey of public governing boards—institutional and system level—shows a relative lack of diversity. Boards, on average, are overwhelmingly male; only 28% of board members are female. Only 23% of board members are racial or ethnic minorities, and 69% of board members are between 50 and 69 years old. Almost half of board members have business backgrounds (Association of Governing Boards [AGB], 2010). Increasing diversity on public higher education boards may be helpful in recruiting a greater diversity of faculty and students.

Autonomy and academic freedom are long-held traditions designed to protect institutions and faculty in the pursuit of knowledge and truth from interference by the government or other outside interests. For example, these concepts indicate that society values a scientist's pursuit of knowledge about man's beginning without pressure from the government or other organizations related to evolution or creationism. For public institutions, certain autonomies and freedoms are granted by the state because the state holds the charter for the institution. The system and institution then determine what autonomies and freedoms are provided to faculty (Johnstone, 2013). Certainly, there are strong professional norms that permeate academic freedom, and one would be hard pressed to find a public institution that did not offer significant freedom to institutions and faculty.

On the other hand, as state centralization and control of higher education grows, institutional autonomy and traditional concepts of faculty governance can be limited. As one higher education scholar notes, "as the locus of influence moves from the campus to the state, public-sector presidents may find themselves becoming more like middle managers than campus leader" (Birnbaum, 1988, p. 16). Faculties' tradition of shared institutional governance on academic, curricular, and peer-related issues, such as the granting of promotion and tenure, may be eroding due to greater pressure on states and institutions to increase the effectiveness and efficiency of higher education. A recent survey of institutional presidents (excluding Bible colleges and seminaries) found that 58% have overruled a department's desire to hire a certain scholar due to questions of the scholar's competence, and 54% have blocked a scholar's tenure for the same reason (Flaherty, 2015). The survey also found that presidents desire even more input into these processes (Flaherty, 2015).

Finance

Higher education finance is just as complicated as, but wholly different from, K–12 and early learning finance. Public institutions of higher education receive funding from the state (through appropriations and student aid), the federal government (through student aid and research grants), and student tuition. Private institutions receive similar funding streams, but much less or no state funding. Both public and private institutions also receive funding from alumni, other donors, foundations, and corporations (National Center for Higher Education Management Systems, 2014). Figure 6.1 provides a graphical depiction of the funding streams to and from colleges and universities.

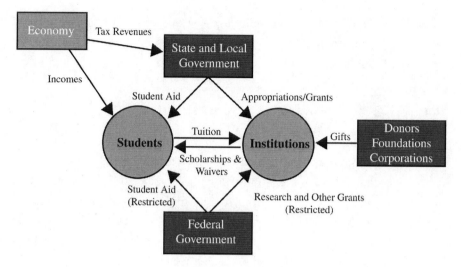

Figure 6.1 Funding streams to and from institutions of higher education.
Source: Reprinted with permission from the National Center for Higher Education Management Systems (2014).

The total amounts of funding and the percentages of funding by source are constant sources of examination and usually consternation. Certainly, as the portion of higher education funding from state sources declines, which will be discussed later, institutions must weigh how much they can increase tuition or donations and/or maintain quality while operating more efficiently. The 2008 economic recession negatively impacted higher education finance. In all but two U.S. states, government spending per student is still below prerecession levels, and at least seven governors are proposing even deeper state funding cuts (Deprez, 2015). Who pays for higher education is not just a monetary issue. The following discussion also centers on societal views about who or what benefits from citizens receiving higher educations. On the one hand, more educated workers are crucial to the current and future economy, as some economists predict that the majority of future job growth will be in areas that require advanced training. On the other hand, it is increasingly clear that individuals with higher education reap significant financial benefits throughout their lifetimes. Who pays for what tends to be a reflection of discussions about whether higher education is primarily a public and/or a private benefit. This values-laden issue should be considered as you read the following section covering major sources of higher education finance including the states, students, institutions, and the federal government.

State

Institutions of higher education are generally funded through formulas, either enrollment based (number of students enrolled) or incremental (previous year allocations adjusted up or down) (Snyder, 2015). Although formulas may call for a certain amount to be distributed to institutions, the formula can only distribute what has been allocated to higher education through the state budget. These amounts have been declining because total state funding for higher education has decreased over the past 30 years (using constant 2013 dollars). Although funding has declined in recent years, states obviously still prioritize higher education; on average, about 13% of states' budgets were spent on this sector (National Association of State Budget Officers, 2014). Per student funding is higher than it was 30 years ago, but lower than 10 years ago (College Board, 2014a). Of course, the economic recession starting in 2008 had a large impact on the ability of states to allocate funding to higher education and other state activities. State and local educational appropriations per student (or full-time equivalent student—FTE) were at a recent high in fiscal year 2008 at $8,081. This dropped to $6,215 two years later and is just now showing a sign of recovery; the fiscal year 2014 figure is $6,552 (SHEEO, 2015). Since the recession, Alabama per-FTE funding took the hardest hit with a decrease of 38.9%, while Illinois was able to increase funding by 50.2% over the same time period (SHEEO, 2015). Across the states, 47.1% of total public higher education revenue is from tuition, which represents a slight decrease from the previous year and a 12 percentage point increase from before the recession (SHEEO, 2015).

A recent survey of system and institutional governing board members found that the number one reason public institutions increase student costs is due to decreased state support. At private institutions, the top reason for increases in student costs is needed capital investments and campus infrastructure (AGB, 2012). Interestingly, 62% of respondents believe that his/her institution generally costs what it should relative to its value, but only

38% believe that higher education in general costs what it should. This pattern is typical in surveys of stakeholders—my school is great, but overall public education is bad; my legislator is great, but Congress is bad. Half of respondents say that their institution does everything it can to reduce expenses (AGB, 2012), which makes one wonder why the other half of respondents are not also doing the same.

Important to the discussion about state funding of higher education is the policy of outcome-based funding. Outcome-based funding, sometimes called performance funding, is a policy mechanism that ties some portion of state higher education funding to outcomes. This was first implemented in Tennessee in 1979, where 2% of state higher education funding was linked to five performance indicators (Bogue & Johnson, 2010). The general theory of action around outcome-based funding is that linking funding to desired goals will encourage institutional prioritization of those goals and ultimately achievement of those goals. Tennessee continues performance funding today, although it has been significantly refined, and many states have followed suit. The 1990s was a popular decade for implementation of such funding mechanisms, but the majority of states adopting formulas during this period eventually abandoned these policies (Dougherty et al., 2014). These ill-fated formulas are often called "1.0 versions" and are characterized by a small percentage of funding attributed to performance, a wide variety of metrics largely linked to institutional rather than state interests, and formula implementation that fluctuated with the economy. Often, the formulas did not differentiate between different types of institutions, such as open access versus research institutions. "This non-differentiation led some institutions to modify their behavior in counterproductive ways to boost their numerical performance on selected metrics (such as limiting access to increase graduation rates)" (Snyder, 2015, p. 5).

Outcome-based funding 2.0 policies started in the late 2000s and are characterized by a greater percentage of the funding formula, narrow metrics tied to state interests such as college completion, and better designed formulas. As of December 2014, 26 states are implementing outcome-based formulas, and 10 additional states are developing such policies (Snyder, 2015). The formulas vary widely by the percentage of funding attributed to performance, the metrics used, and differentiation between types of institutions (Snyder, 2015).

To date, there has been much more research on 1.0 outcome-based formulas because they have been in place longer. Generally, this research finds
little empirical evidence that the formulas helped institutions or states meet
stated goals (see, for example, Shin, 2010; Shin & Milton, 2004; Tandberg,
et al., 2014). Effects of 2.0 versions of outcome-based funding on stated
goals has yet to be studied in depth, but policy leaders are hoping that the
differences in the 2.0 formulas will make them more effective.

Related to outcome-based funding, which attempts to incentivize concrete results, is a movement toward trying to measure student learning.
Right now, graduation is the major proxy for student learning under the
assumption that faculty carefully design programs of study for each major
and would not pass students from a course if the requisite knowledge was
not obtained. However, there are increasing attempts to more accurately
measure student knowledge to gauge progress from year to year, at certain
milestones, and upon completion.

Students

Unlike public early learning and K–12 education, students (and their families) share the cost for higher education, whether it is at a public or private
institution. These costs have been an increasingly popular topic in the media
as student costs appear to be rising. According to the latest trends in college
pricing report by the College Board, "College price increases are not accel-
erating. But they are accumulating" (2014a, p. 7).

What does it cost to attend college? The most recent figures show that the
average annual in-state undergraduate tuition and fees for full-time students
at public four-year institutions amount to $8,070 per year. An extra $9,404
is estimated for living and other expenses. Average out-of-state tuition and
fees are substantially higher than in-state costs at $22,603. Average tuition
and fees for private institutions are $25,696, and in-state tuition at two-year
colleges costs $2,882 (National Center for Education Statistics, 2015). It is
important to note that these are averages for all types of institutions. Tuition
and fees at very selective research institutions may be much higher than at
more open access institutions.

Tuition setting for public institutions is a multistep process that usually
begins in the fall and continues through the spring. It includes consideration

of revenue projections from sources other than students and anticipated costs (Carlson, 2013). The process may include several leaders, namely the state's governor, legislature, statewide coordinating or governing board, local district governing boards, and/or individual institutions (Carlson, 2013). If there are several participants, each may have a different role in tuition setting. For example, the governor, legislature, or board may have full legal decision-making authority, while others will have informal or consultative roles. In 21 states, the coordinating or governing board has full legal decision-making authority for tuition setting at four-year schools (Carlson, 2013). The collaborative approach may help to keep costs down; unsurprisingly, research has found that if individual institutions have sole discretion in setting tuition rates, the rates are likely to increase (Kim & Ko, 2014).

It is important to recognize the distinction between "sticker price" tuition and what students actually pay, or "net tuition." Often, institutions will discount the advertised tuition price to attract certain types of excellent students or to help students in need. Other types of state and/or federal aid can defray tuition costs as well. The bottom line is what students and their families must pay out of pocket. Research by the College Board has found that

> on average, in 2011–12, full-time in-state students at public four-year universities from families with incomes below $30,000 received enough grant aid to cover tuition and fees and have about $2,320 left to put toward room, board, and other expenses.
>
> (2014a, p. 25)

However, the room, board, and other living expenses are estimated to be $13,340, and the extra money from grants and aid only covers a fraction of that amount. This is what concerns many policymakers and analysts—that many low-income students, as opposed to wealthier students, must work while in college, take out loans to supplement grant aid, or choose not to attend college at all. It is important to have a basic understanding of higher education funding because it affects other higher education policies such as college enrollment and attainment. The rest of this section will provide more detail about student aid and loans.

There are many types of student aid: scholarships and grants from the institution or external organization, merit aid from the state, need-based aid from the state or the federal government, loans from the state or federal government, and work/study arrangements. For graduate students, teaching or research assistantships often provide a nominal salary and cover the cost of tuition. Table 6.2 depicts the types of state student financial assistance programs.

The most recent figures show that the majority of aid (54%) given to undergraduates was in the form of grants. Thirty-seven percent of aid was in the form of loans and 9% of aid was in a combination of tax credits or deductions and federal work-study opportunities. For graduate students, the greater share of aid was in loans (62%), then grants (32%), and finally tax credits, deductions, and work-study (6%) (College Board, 2014b). "In 2013–14, 40% of all grant aid came from the federal government, 39% from colleges and universities, 13% from employers and other private sources, and 8% from state governments" (College Board, 2014b, p. 3).

It is not surprising that the largest amount of grant aid comes from the federal government, given its support of the Pell Grant program. This program has provided need-based aid to undergraduate students since the Higher Education Act of 1965. Thirty-eight percent of undergraduate students, or

Table 6.2   Types of State Student Financial Assistance Programs

	Offered under state statute	Offered through a formal policy but not in statute	Offered at discretion of institutions	Not offered
Need-based grants	22	6	3	2
Merit-based grants	20	2	9	2
Blended program (need and merit)	8	2	8	10
Work-study	7	2	10	11
Categorical program targeted at a specific population	24	3	4	1

Source: Carlson (2013), p. 20.

9.2 million students, received a Pell Grant in 2013–14. This represents an increase from 25% of undergraduates in 2003–04 (College Board, 2014b). Grant amounts are provided on a sliding scale. Only undergraduate students with an expected family contribution of zero and who enroll in school full time receive the maximum annual grant of $5,730 (for the 2014–15 school year). Twenty-seven percent of Pell Grant recipients earn the maximum award. The maximum grant covers 63% of average public four-year tuition and fees. This is down from 79% 10 years ago. The average Pell Grant per student is $3,678, and total federal expenditures on this program are $33.7 billion (College Board, 2014b).

States also give a substantial amount of aid to students. State approaches differ widely as some states only give aid based on merit, some states only give aid based on financial need, and other states give a combination of aid. The argument for need-based aid is clear—to help those students who might not otherwise go to college because of financial reasons. The arguments for merit-based aid are different, but also compelling. Offering the state's "best and brightest" students with financial assistance to attend a state college maintains a steady pipeline of talented students into state institutions and increases the likelihood that those students will stay in state once they graduate. Research supports this proposition (Zhang & Ness, 2010).

Fourteen states have merit-based aid programs and most are in the southeast region (Zhang & Ness, 2010). Most merit-based aid programs require a certain grade point average upon high school graduation and a minimum score on a college entrance exam like the SAT or ACT (Delaney & Ness, forthcoming). Recent data indicate that 75% of all state aid was in the form of need-based grants, and 23 states allocate the vast majority of their state aid to students in need (College Board, 2014b). State grant aid per student also varies by state. South Carolina offers the most per student at $1,890 (College Board, 2014b).

Although much has been made in recent years about the increasing debt load of students, recent data from the College Board indicate that the outlook may not be as bleak as once thought. Since 2007–08, the portion of all undergraduate aid in the form of loans has been decreasing (College Board, 2014b). "The reality is that students *are* leaving school with more debt than their counterparts five or ten years ago. Moreover, because the number of people going to college has increased significantly over the past decade, the total amount borrowed each year and the total amount of outstanding debt have grown much faster than individual debt levels" (College Board, 2014b, p. 7). Still, the majority of graduates earn both a diploma and loan debt. About 60% of four-year college graduates carry some debt at an average amount of $27,300, an increase of 19% over the past decade. Sixty-nine percent of borrowers with outstanding education debt owed $25,000 or less. Nine percent of borrowers with outstanding federal loans were in default as of fall 2013, and the defaults constituted only 5% of all total outstanding debt. For-profit institutions accounted for nearly half the students who defaulted on their loans. Twenty-four percent of defaults came from students who attended public two-year colleges, 20% from public four-year institutions, and 10% from private nonprofit four-year colleges (College Board, 2014b). Interestingly, recent research from the federal reserve bank of New York found that student loan defaults decrease with a higher loan balance. Thirty-four percent of students who owed $5,000 or less defaulted on their loans, while only 18% of students who owed $100,001 or more defaulted on their loans ("Data Point," 2015).

Student defaults are not the only issue regarding loans. Since the federal government is again providing direct loans to students, there have been many complaints about the system. In early 2015, President Obama announced the creation of a Student Bill of Rights program which will include creation of a centralized complaint system for federal student loan borrowers and a single web site for managing loan payments. The president also plans to "convene an interagency task force to develop regulatory and legislative proposals to help struggling borrowers with both federal and private student loans" (Stratford, 2015b).

Institutions

Other than state financial support and basic student tuition revenues, institutions support themselves through endowments and tinkering with the balance of out-of-state and/or international students.

Both public and private institutions utilize endowments to fund a myriad of costs including new dorms, building construction, salaries, and tuition

aid for low-income students (Upton & Schnaars, 2012). In 2012, 837 institutions reported having an endowment (Upton & Schnaars, 2012). Harvard
University has the largest endowment overall at $36.4 billion (Rivard,
2014) and the University of Texas has the largest endowment for a public school (Upton & Schnaars, 2012). Overall, endowment funds for all
institutions have been rising, with double-digit returns the past two years
(Rivard, 2014). With these significant stores of money, one might wonder
why institutions of higher education are not able to fund all of their needs.
The issue is that the principal of the endowment is usually protected,
and only the interest may be spent each year. Average reported spending rates for college and university endowments in 2012–13 was between
4% and 5% (College Board, 2014a). Another limiting factor on endowment
expenditures is the purpose for which money donated to the institution
was earmarked. Many donors specify a certain project or target for their
donation, which limits the college or university's spending discretion.

Another source of funding for public institutions comes from premium
tuition prices. Traditionally, out-of-state and international students pay
a premium for attending public institutions because the state only sub-
sidizes tuition for its citizens. Many elite private institutions in the U.S.
do not charge a premium to international students, so this section focuses
on public institutions. The extra funding public institutions receive from
out-of-state and international students can help bolster revenues. Not sur-
prisingly, a study of public institutions from 2000 to 2012 showed that
the percentage of in-state residents constituting the freshman class is, on
average, decreasing. Of more than 400 public colleges and universities,
60% saw a decline in the percentage of in-state freshmen. One-fifth of
the institutions saw a drop of 10 or more percentage points. Particularly
notable was the University of Alabama, which went from 75% in-state
enrollment for its 2000 freshman class to only 45% in 2012 (Burd, 2015).
Some state leaders are attempting to modify this institutional behavior
by proposing extra funding for in-state students or capping the number
of out-of-state and international students (Burd, 2015). Considering the
public nature of these institutions and that many of them have land-grant
status, it is interesting that their service to the state, in the way of student
seats, is dwindling.

Federal Government

Although the federal government's role in financing higher education has been discussed in other portions of this section, there are a few additional points to note. Overall, the federal government financially supports higher education through purchasing research and development services, meeting special needs (e.g., college library support), and providing funding directly to students and families (Gladieux, King, & Corrigan, 2005). Federal sources of funding account for 34% of total institutional revenue at a public doctoral institution but only 14% at a two-year public institution (College Board, 2014a). Most of this difference is likely due to research support at four-year and graduate institutions.

The federal government plays a large role in financially supporting research at colleges and universities. Universities conducted slightly over half of federally funded basic research in 2012. Federal funding constituted 61% of all basic research support at universities. Although high, this percentage has decreased since 1965, when the federal government research support made up 77% of university research funding (Association of American Universities [AAU], 2015). Universities themselves are now supporting a greater percentage of research. Most federal research grants to universities come from the National Institutes of Health and the National Science Foundation, and most research funding is geared toward life and physical sciences. Funding for social science research was only at 1.7% of total federal funding for university basic research (AAU, 2015).

Shortly after President Lyndon Johnson left office, he reflected on the significant financial support—namely, research and financial aid funding— initiated for higher education during his terms in office. He noted,

> Let us not begrudge the costs of these programs. The funds we provide do not simply disappear, never to be recovered. A highly educated population creates far more wealth than it consumes. Our experience with the GI Bill proved that, once and for all.
>
> (Johnson, 1969, p. 109)

It appears that presidential administrations succeeding President Johnson, whether Democrat or Republican, seem to agree.

Major Stakeholders

There are many organizations and associations supporting and advocating for higher education and its various components and groups. These organizations can be categorized into three groups: groups with an evaluative role (e.g., accrediting bodies), groups with an affiliate role (e.g., professional membership organizations), and groups with a funding role (e.g., foundations) (Hendrickson et al., 2013). This section will provide some discussion on accrediting bodies and professional membership organizations. Foundations were extensively covered in the K–12 chapter and are also influential in higher education, but the discussion remains very similar to that in the K–12 section and is therefore not repeated here.

Accrediting agencies began in the late 1800s out of a need for standards in the absence of a national centralizing body (Hendrickson et al., 2013). Accreditors assess, usually through peer review, institutions, colleges, and departments according to predefined standards. There are six regional accrediting bodies as well as several other specialized and professional accrediting agencies. Overall,

> accreditation is intended to ensure quality in the academic offerings of an institution and the fiscal stability to sustain them; provide access to federal funding since the government will provide student financial aid or other programmatic resources only to recognized accredited institutions; engender private sector confidence by ensuring to prospective employers a proper level of credentialing; and ensure quality to facilitate the transfer of credits between institutions.
>
> (Hendrickson et al., 2013, p. 206, text from Eaton, 2011)

American higher education associations sometimes act in concert and are often referred to as the "One Dupont" group—because many of them share the same address in Washington, DC (One Dupont Circle). The American Council of Education (ACE), founded in 1918, acts as the umbrella organization for several of these higher education associations. It represents public and private two- and four-year institutions and purports to "coordinate the advocacy efforts of the entire community." It coordinates 50 educational associations known as the Washington Higher Education Secretariat, which meets monthly in Washington, DC, to discuss higher education issues of common interest (Harcleroad & Eaton, 2005). Some members of the secretariat include the Association of Public and Land-Grant Universities, the National Association of Independent Colleges and Universities, and the American Association of Community Colleges.

Another important advocacy group is the Association of Governing Boards of Universities and Colleges, which represents 34,500 trustees of nearly 1,800 colleges and universities and their related foundations. Other than advocacy groups, regional compacts are very important to state higher education policy. There are four regional compacts, including the Western Interstate Commission for Higher Education, the New England Board of Higher Education, the Midwestern Higher Education Compact, and the Southern Regional Education Board. Three of them were established shortly after World War II and all of them help states address educational issues that transcended state lines. Forty-six states are members of a regional compact (Harcleroad & Eaton, 2005).

Major Policy Issues

Similar to the major policy issues sections in other chapters, there are myriad higher education policy topics that could be explored. Here I have chosen to examine policies on who goes to college and who completes college. Not only do these topics capture the span of higher education access and success, but they are also central to current policy debates occurring within and among higher education institutions, government leaders, advocacy organizations, foundations, and researchers.

College for All: Who Should Attend?

Many policy leaders at all levels of government are touting the need for a more educated workforce and hence the need for more students to complete a postsecondary credential such as a certificate or degree. For more students to complete, more students need to enter the pipeline beyond what conventional population growth provides. In some policy circles, this has manifested into a "college for all" approach, a policy argument undergirded by both economic and equity rationales. The economic rationale is that more educated workers are needed. Some labor economists suggest that the American economy will need 20 million additional postsecondary-educated workers by 2025 (Carnevale & Rose, 2011).

The equity rationale highlights the college enrollment and attainment gaps between racial, ethnic, and socioeconomic student groups and strives to eliminate those gaps by disrupting current patterns and calling for educators and leaders to assume that all students can and should attend college. The equity gaps are important based upon the individual benefits that accrue from earning a postsecondary credential, namely a decreased chance of unemployment and higher earnings.

Although unemployment at all education levels has decreased over the past three years, gaps remain between levels of educational attainment. For instance, recent high school diploma holders have a 17.8% unemployment rate, whereas recent college graduates have a 7.5% rate (Carnevale & Cheah, 2015).

Educational attainment significantly affects individual earning potential. Over a lifetime, someone with a bachelor's degree will typically earn $1.2 million, which is double what a typical high school graduate would earn (Hershbein & Kearney, 2014). One researcher found that the earnings gap between high school and college graduates has more than doubled over the past 30 years and that "about two-thirds of the overall rise of earnings dispersion between 1980 and 2005 is proximately accounted for by the increased premium associated with schooling in general and postsecondary education in particular" (Autor, 2014, p. 843). Not surprisingly, the premium for a college degree varies by major. One study found the premium for a college degree over a high school education was highest for engineers at 138% and was lowest for arts, recreation, psychology, and social work majors at 29% (Carnevale & Cheah, 2015).

This has led to calls for rigorous high school curriculums for all students that eliminate traditional vocational and college-prep tracks. While this does indeed promote equity, it may prompt other critical questions such as why all students must take Algebra II regardless of their intended career path. A common answer to this type of question is that secondary school students are too young to know definitively what career paths are ahead of them, and perhaps their conceptions of career paths are influenced by cultural or other limitations. Ensuring that all students have a rigorous curriculum ensures no student is tracked based on prejudices or bias (however unintended) or is limited by his/her own imagination. The "college for all" policy seems to be in a state of flux while policy leaders try to simultaneously ensure an educated workforce, equitable access to rigorous learning, and common sense approaches to meeting students' unique learning needs and ambitions.

College Completion

While college access has been and remains a top policy focus, college completion rates have recently come under scrutiny. Up until recently, policy leaders and society at large seemed to leave college success and completion to the student. As discussed earlier in this chapter in the context of President Obama's initiatives, the economic imperative for a more educated workforce has shined a new light on the efficiency of higher education institutions in graduating students. This seems to be working, as 94% of responding members of institutional and system higher education governing boards believe that colleges and universities need to do more to increase the percentage of enrolled students who complete degrees (AGB, 2012).

The federal government began tracking overall college completion rates with the 1996 freshman cohort. Just under 34% of that cohort of first-time, full-time, bachelor's degree–seeking students at four-year institutions graduated in four years (National Center for Education Statistics, 2015). The rate increased slightly to 39% with the 2007 entering cohort. If the graduation date is stretched to five years to allow for changes in majors, internships, study abroad experiences, and other reasons for delay, the graduation rate was 55%, and at six years it was 59% (National Center for Education Statistics, 2015).

Within the overall completion rates, the data show some disparities among types of institutions and student characteristics. Nonprofit institutions have the highest graduation rates at 52.8%. Females graduate at a higher rate than males—44% compared to 35%. More selective institutions have higher graduation rates as institutions with less than a 25% acceptance rate had an average graduation rate of 89%, while open access institutions had a rate of 34% in six years (National Center for Education Statistics, 2015). A student's family income may also affect his/her likelihood of graduating college. Calculations conducted by The Pell Institute and PennAHEAD (2015) found that in 2013, 21% of entering students in the bottom quartile of family income graduated college after entering, and 99% of students in the top quartile of family income did the same. Other researchers caution that while there may indeed be disparities in completion rates by family income level, the data used for this study, and data availability in general to make these types of inferences, are far from perfect. Chingos and Dynarski (2015) argue that it is more likely that 65%, rather than 99%, of entering students from families with incomes in the top quartile complete college.

Whether or not a student is prepared to succeed in college has a large impact on the student's success. Many students are delayed in taking credit-earning courses because, although they graduated from high school, they are not yet ready to take college-level courses. Colleges, mostly at the open access and lower selectivity levels, have offered remediation to such students. Of undergraduate students entering college in the fall of 2011, almost 20% took one or more remedial class during their first year (National Center for Education Statistics, 2015). The largest percentage of students taking remedial classes was at two-year institutions, but the rate was only marginally higher than the percentage of students needing remediation at public, four-year, nondoctoral institutions (National Center for Education Statistics, 2015). Research consistently shows that students taking remediation education complete college at much lower rates than those students who do not require remediation. These dismal statistics have generated new structural designs for remediation, such as offering it simultaneously with core classes. This has also put more pressure on K–12 and higher education to collaborate in ensuring high school graduation requirements align with basic college entry expectations.

Looking Forward

Going forward, the higher education landscape may change dramatically. Increasing pressures on the sector will manifest in one way or another. Certainly, the financial pressures that both institutions and students are facing will require structural changes. The pattern of decreasing state funding leading to higher student tuition cannot continue its trajectory indefinitely, especially given the imperative to help more students earn postsecondary credentials. Innovations are occurring, but it is unclear whether any of them will solve the push and pull between finances and production. For instance, massive open online courses allow anyone in the world to take a web-based college course for free. Although college credit is typically not offered, a certificate of completion usually is, which could be a signal to future employers of knowledge and competency. This type of learning and credentialing has not yet become mainstream. On a smaller scale, higher education institutions are trying to reduce the costs to students for books and materials by encouraging faculty to take advantage of the wealth of materials on the Internet. Professors are reshaping syllabi to include primary source materials (e.g., a government or historical document), videos, and other web-based resources rather than relying solely on a hard-copy textbook.

As these innovations are occurring, state and federal governments are looking for more accountability from institutions for student learning outcomes, costs, research productivity, and other metrics. Ultimately, government leaders want to ensure that a quality education is being produced at an efficient rate, and they want to provide transparent information to students and families who are increasingly being seen as consumers of higher education.

The federal government may have a sizeable impact on the future of the higher education landscape as leaders work on the reauthorization of the Higher Education Act. With a focus on reducing institutional regulations, managing student costs, and increasing educational attainment, this law could shape institutional and state behavior in many ways. Ultimately, it will be interesting to see whether the push for greater educational attainment will produce workers with the skills and knowledge needed for the future economy. Can the U.S. system of higher education attract and retain a more diverse student body? Will students self-select into the programs and majors that will lead to the jobs of the future? Will a new social contract develop around who finances higher education? And will all of this result in the U.S. maintaining or increasing its globally competitive advantage?

For Further Information

- *The Chronicle of Higher Education* is a weekly newspaper dedicated to the higher education sector: www.chronicle.com

- *Inside Higher Ed* is a daily higher education newsletter: www.insidehigh ered.com
- The National Center for Higher Education Management Systems is a nonprofit organization that supplies data and information on higher education: www.nchems.org
- Grapevine provides an annual compilation of data on state support for higher education: http://education.illinoisstate.edu/grapevine/
- The Integrated Postsecondary Education Data System (IPEDS) is part of the National Center for Education Statistics and provides a data inter- face that is accessible to those looking for basic information and those wanting to conduct more sophisticated statistical methods: https://nces. ed.gov/ipeds/

Notes

1. Higher education is sometimes referred to as postsecondary education. Both terms will be used interchangeably in this chapter.
2. www.aaup.org/issues/tenure

References

American Association of State Colleges and Universities. (2015, March). *The 2015 gubernatorial state of the state addresses and higher education.* Retrieved from www. aascu.org/policy/state-policy/2015StateoftheStates.pdf

Aragon, S. & Rowland, J. (2015, February). *Governors' top education issues: 2015 state of the state addresses.* Retrieved from www.ecs.org/clearinghouse/01/17/60/11760.pdf

Association of American Universities (AAU). (2015, February). *Basic scientific and engineering research at U.S. universities.* Retrieved from www.aau.edu

Association of Governing Boards of Universities and Colleges (AGB). (2010). *Poli- cies, practices, and composition of governing boards of public colleges, universities, and systems.* Retrieved from http://agb.org/reports/2010/2010-policies-practices-and-com position-governing-boards-public-colleges-universities-a

Association of Governing Boards of Universities and Colleges. (2012). *The 2012 AGB survey of higher education governance—college prices, costs, and outcomes.* Retrieved from http://agb.org/reports/2012/2012-agb-survey-higher-education-governance

Autor, D. (2014). Skills, education, and the rise of earnings inequality among the "other 99 percent". *Science, 344*(6186), 843–851. doi:10.1126/science.1251868

Birnbaum, R. (1988). *How colleges work.* San Francisco, CA: Jossey-Bass.

Bogue, E., & Johnson, D. (2010). Performance incentives and public college accountability in the United States: A quarterly century policy audit. *Higher Education and Management Policy, 22*(2), 1–22.

Burd, S. (2015, March 11). Are public universities becoming bastions of privilege? *The Hechinger Report.* Retrieved from http://hechingerreport.org/public-universities-becoming-bastions-privilege/

Carey, K. (2014, November 29). For accomplished students, reaching a good college isn't as hard as it seems. *The New York Times.* Retrieved from www.nytimes.com

Carlson, A. (2013, September 16). *State tuition, fees, and financial assistance policies for public colleges and universities, 2012–13.* Retrieved from www.sheeo.org/resources/publications/state-tuition-fees-and-financial-assistance-policies

Carnevale, A., & Cheah, B. (2015). *From hard times to better times: College majors, unemployment, and earnings.* Retrieved from www.cew.georgetown.edu

Carnevale, A., & Rose, S. (2011). *The undereducated American.* Retrieved from https://cew.georgetown.edu/report/the-undereducated-american/

Chingos, M., & Dynarski, S. (2015, March 12). *How can we track trends in educational attainment by parental income? Hint: not with the current population survey.* Retrieved from www.brookings.edu/research/papers/2015/03/12-chalkboard-income-education-attainment-chingos

College Board. (2014a). *Trends in college pricing 2014.* Retrieved from www.trends.collegeboard.org

College Board. (2014b). *Trends in student aid 2014.* Retrieved from www.trends.collegeboard.org

Data Point: Behind the numbers in the news. (2015, March 20). *The Chronicle of Higher Education,* p. A31.

Delaney, J. A., & Ness, E. C. (in press). Creating a merit aid typology. In B. Curs (Ed.), *Merit aid reconsidered. New directions in institutional research.* San Francisco, CA: Jossey-Bass.

Deprez, E. (2015, March 5). States are slashing college budgets and raising tuition. Bloomberg. Retrieved from: http://finance.yahoo.com/news/states-slashing-college-budgets-raising-120013344.html

Dougherty, D., Jones, S., Lahr, H., Natow, R., Pheatt, L., & Reddy, V. (2014). Performance funding for higher education: Forms, origins, impacts, and futures. *The Annals of the American Academy of Political and Social Science, 655,* 163–184.

Eaton, J. (2011). An overview of U.S. accreditation. Washington, D.C.: Council for Higher Education Accreditation. Retrieved from http://chea.org/pdf/Overview%20of%20US%20Accreditation%2003.2011.pdf

Education Commission of the States. (2014). *Postsecondary governance database.* Retrieved from www.ecs.org/html/educationIssues/Governance/GovPSDB_intro.asp

Fain, P. (2015, March 26). Enrollment woes continue for U. of Phoenix. *Inside Higher Education.* Retrieved from www.insidehighered.com

Field, K. (2014, December 19). Obama's college-ratings plan arrives, but most specifics stay behind. *Chronicle of Higher Education*. Retrieved from www.chronicle.com

Field, K. (2015, January 20). 6 years in and 6 to go, only modest progress on Obama's college-completion goal. *Chronicle of Higher Education*. Retrieved from www.chronicle.com

Flaherty, C. (2015, March 13). Presidents say they want more input in faculty hiring and tenure decisions. *Inside Higher Education*. Retrieved from www.insidehighered.com

Gladieux, L., King, J., & Corrigan, M. (2005). The federal government and higher education. In P. Altbach, R. Berdahl, & P. Gumport (Eds.), *American higher education in the twenty-first century* (2nd ed., pp. 163–197). Baltimore, MD: The Johns Hopkins University Press.

Harcleroad, F., & Eaton, J. (2005). The hidden hand: External constituencies and their impact. In P. Altbach, R. Berdahl, & P. Gumport (Eds.), *American higher education in the twenty-first century* (2nd ed., pp. 253–286). Baltimore, MD: The Johns Hopkins University Press.

Hauptman, A. (2013). U.S. attainment rates, demographics, and the supply of college graduates. *Change: The Magazine of Higher Learning, 43*(3), 24–33.

Hendrickson, R., Lane, J., Harris, J., & Dorman, R. (2013). *Academic leadership and governance of higher education*. Sterling, VA: Stylus.

Hershbein, B., & Kearney, M. (2014, September 30). *Major decisions: What graduates earn over their lifetimes*. Retrieved from www.hamiltonproject.org/papers

Immerwahr, J., & Johnson, J. (2009). *Squeeze play 2009: The public's views on college costs today*. Retrieved from www.publicagenda.org/pages/squeeze-play-2009

Johnson, L. (1969). The choices we face. New York, NY: Bantam Books.

Johnstone, D. (2013). Higher educational autonomy and the apportionment of authority among state governments, public multi-campus systems, and member colleges and universities. In J. Lane and D. Johnstone (Eds.), *Higher education systems 3.0* (pp. 75–100) Albany, NY: SUNY Press.

Kim, M., & Ko, J. (2014). The impacts of state control policies on college tuition increases. *Educational Policy*. Advance online publication. doi:10.1177/0895904813518100

Knott, J., & Payne, A. (2004). The impact of state governance structures on management and performance of public organizations: A study of higher education institutions. *Journal of Policy Analysis and Management, 23*, 13–30.

Mangan, K., & Supiano, B. (2014, December 19). More metrics, more problems: Breaking down Obama's college-ratings plan. *Chronicle of Higher Education*. Retrieved from www.chronicle.com

McGuinness, Jr. A. (2005). The States and Higher Education. In P. Altbach, R. Berdahl & P. Gumport, (Eds.) *American Higher Education in the Twenty-First*

Century: Social, Political, and Economic Challenges 2nd *edition*. The Johns Hopkins University Press: Baltimore.

McGuinness, A. (2013). Serving public purposes: Challenges for systems in changing state contexts. In J. Lane and D. Johnstone (Eds.), *Higher education systems 3.0* (pp. 193–214). Albany, NY: SUNY Press.

McLendon, M., & Ness, E. (2003). The politics of state higher education governance reform. *Peabody Journal of Education, 78*, 66–88.

National Association of State Budget Officers. (2014, November 20). *State expenditure report.* Retrieved from www.nasbo.org/sites/default/files/Summary_State%20Expenditure%20Report.pdf

National Center for Education Statistics. (2015). *Digest of education statistics.* Retrieved from www.nces.ed.gov

National Center for Higher Education Management Systems. (2014). *Finance: Diagram.* Retrieved from www.higheredinfo.org/catcontent/cat8.php

Nicholson-Crotty, J., & Meier, K. (2004). Politics, Structure, and Public Policy: The Case of Higher Education. *Educational Policy, 17*, 80–96.

OECD. (2014). *Education at a glance 2014* (chart C3.2). Retrieved from http://dx.doi.org/10.1787/888933118599

The Pell Institute & PennAHEAD. *Indicators of higher education equity in the United States.* (2015). Retrieved from www.pellinstitute.org/downloads/publications-Indicators_of_Higher_Education_Equity_in_the_US_45_Year_Trend_Report.pdf

Quality counts report: Chance of success. (2014, January 9). *Education Week.* Retrieved from www.edweek.org/ew/toc/2014/01/09/index.html

Rivard, R. (2014, September 30). College endowment funds likely had another year of double-digit returns. *Inside Higher Education.* Retrieved from www.insidehighered.com

Shin, J. (2010). Impacts of performance-based accountability on institutional performance in the U.S. *Higher Education, 60*, 47–68.

Shin, J., & Milton, S. (2004). Effects of performance budgeting and funding programs on graduation rates in public four-year colleges and universities. *Education Policy Analysis Archives, 12*(22), 1–26.

Snyder, M. (2015, February). *Driving better outcomes: Typology and principles to inform outcomes-based funding models.* Retrieved from http://hcmstrategists.com/maximizingresources/

State Higher Education Executive Officers (SHEEO). (2015). *State higher education finance FY2014.* Retrieved from www.sheeo.org/projects/shef-%E2%80%94-state-higher-education-finance

Stratford, M. (2015a, February 25). Alexander says Congress will pass Higher Ed Act this year, backs plan to cut regulations on colleges. *Inside Higher Education.* Retrieved from www.insidehighered.com

Stratford, M. (2015b, March 10). Obama administration will create student loan complaint system, centralized payments for borrows. *Inside Higher Education.* Retrieved from www.insidehighered.com

Tandberg, D., Hillman, N., & Barakat, M. (2014). State higher education performance funding for community colleges: Diverse effects and policy implications. *Teachers College Record, 116*(120307), 1–31.

Thelin, J. (2004). *A history of American higher education.* Baltimore, MD: The Johns Hopkins University Press.

Trustees of Dartmouth College v. Woodward, 17 U.S. 518 (1819).

Upton, J., & Schnaars, C. (2012, September 9). Endowments fund dorms, salaries—and sometimes tuition. *USA Today.* Retrieved from http://usatoday30.usatoday.com/news/education/story/2012-09-09/where-endowment-money-goes/57704440/1

Williams, R. (1991). *The origins of federal support for higher education.* University Park: The Pennsylvania State University Press.

Zhang, L., & Ness, E. (2010). Does state merit-based aid stem brain drain? *Educational Evaluation and Policy Analysis, 32*(2), 143–165.

Part III

TOOLS FOR CONTINUED LEARNING

Chapter 7

Development and Uses of Educational Research

This book has presented a good deal of information on American education policy, much of which was derived from educational research studies. In fact, one of the unique aspects of this book is its utilization of education research and data to provide an overview of education policy concepts in a manner that most professional people can understand. As will be discussed further in this chapter, it is unfortunate that use of education research in this manner is in fact unique. This chapter will examine several facets of educational research and its connection to educational policymaking, such as: What is research? Who conducts education research? Who uses it? What are the connections between researchers and policymakers? First, the unique issues surrounding connections between education research and policymaking will be introduced. Then, a short primer on types of research will be presented. Finally, the chapter will focus on the supply and demand for research regarding education policymaking.

Many policymakers lament the perceived lack of relevant, digestible research that can be used to inform current education policy issues. Many researchers lament policymakers' perceived ignorance of or refusal to use available education research. As with most things, the truth probably lies somewhere in the middle of these two generalized perceptions. Without a doubt, education research should be an integral part of policymaking, and how the two fields should be connected has long been a source of consternation and reflection. The only thing known for sure is that making connections between policymakers and researchers is not simple. Lubienski, Scott, and DeBray (2014) perhaps best describe the issues in applying education research to education policy problems. They cite the following four characteristics of this policy field that contribute to the inability of policymakers to grab and use "off-the-shelf" research for policymaking:

1.   There are unclear or indirect causal relationships between policy inputs and consequences for the wider community, thus leaving substantial uncertainty around research claims about specific interventions.
2.   The costs of policy interventions are more clearly specified for individuals than are individual benefits.
3.   There are substantial resources at stake, thus inviting attention from private interests through political channels.
4.   There are multiple producers of research evidence—including universities, labor unions, think tanks, advocacy groups, and trade associations, for example. (p. 135)

Although Lubienski et al. clearly describe the inherent difficulties in applying education research to education policy, there are potentially other reasons connections are not made, including inability to access and/or understand academic research studies and the politicization of policy. No matter what the reason, almost all can agree that it would be beneficial for education policy to foster more communication between researchers and policymakers. Frederick Hess (2008) provides a good example of what can happen when this communication does not happen or happens poorly. A 1980s study of class size in Tennessee found that smaller kindergarten and first grade classes produced student achievement gains. California state legislators learned of these gains and allocated billions of dollars to reduce class sizes across California. Unfortunately, studies found this effort did not affect student achievement in

California, and these scarce resources were wasted. The California policy-makers did not endeavor to understand the context of the Tennessee study and made the faulty assumption that what worked in Tennessee would work in California. Further, California legislators changed some aspects of the Tennessee program, such as using larger class sizes than in Tennessee, and implemented it on a much larger scale than Tennessee did. Context, experiment design, and scalability are all factors that may seem irrelevant to policymakers, but they are actually important in translating research to policy and programs. This may frustrate policymakers because it leaves little room for a bright line "this works" or "that doesn't," but as Hess (2008) notes,

> many of the biggest controversies in education . . . relate to governance, management, compensation, and deregulation. These policies are rarely precise and do not take place in controlled circumstances. Research can shed light on how such reforms unfold and how context matters, but it is unlikely to determine with any surety whether such policies 'work'.
>
> (p. 2)

Still, research has been used to shape education policies. Perhaps most notably, research on the ramifications of racial stigma on academic achievement contributed to the *Brown v. Board of Education* (1954) decisions outlawing racial segregation in public schools (Lubienski, Scott, & DeBray, 2014). Educational research was later instrumental in designing the education portions of President Johnson's Great Society programs (Hess, 2008; Ness, 2010). This spurred even greater demand for educational research, and in 1972, President Nixon established the National Institute of Education to fund and conduct education research studies. President Reagan dissolved the agency in 1980, but it was reestablished in 2002 as the Institute of Education Sciences with the aim of undertaking scientific education research, which was foundational to the federal No Child Left Behind programs (Murnane & Willett, 2011).

Types of Research

The definition of research may vary by person and situation. On one end of the spectrum, some may conceive of research as any type of information that sheds light on an issue, including personal anecdotes, media reports, surveys, and statistics. On the other end, research can be interpreted very narrowly to only include studies conducted in a scientific manner. Anecdotal and other related types of information are very important to the shaping of policy, but this chapter will focus on the supply of and demand for more empirical and scientific research. Technical or descriptive research is the most basic. It presents basic data without much analysis. For example, descriptive research may include a report on class sizes by school or district, notations of education statements in governors' state of the state addresses, or a calculation of the percent of a state's four-year-olds living in poverty. It is often produced by government agencies, as they are the ones collecting the data.

Scientific research is a "gold standard" because it goes beyond descriptive data to try to determine whether, how, why, or to what extent something happens. Scientific researchers strive to eliminate personal bias and other confounding factors to study the relationship between two or more variables or understand phenomena. Scientific research is usually peer reviewed by other academics in a "blind" manner, meaning that the reviewers do not know who wrote the paper and authors do not know who reviewed it. Acceptance into top-tier academic journals is very competitive, and usually only the most rigorous research is accepted for publication. Very often, if a paper is not rejected outright, reviewers note issues and make suggestions and the author has to revise and resubmit the paper for publication.

Scientific research can be described as qualitative or quantitative. Qualitative research attempts to understand meaning, potentially answering why and how rather than what. Merriam (2009) states that qualitative research is "interested in understanding how people interpret their experiences, how they construct their worlds, and what meaning they attribute to their experiences" (p. 5). Qualitative research follows the scientific method by purposefully choosing the subject and methods of study and carefully following a research protocol. Researchers analyze the data collected through qualitative studies by identifying recurring patterns (Merriam, 2009, p. 23). Results are often characterized by rich descriptions of the phenomenon being studied (Merriam, 2009). Examples of qualitative research methods include case studies, ethnography, and historical research.

Quantitative research employs statistical analysis on defined data sets. This can range from simple correlations between two variables to highly sophisticated techniques such as network analysis and multiple regressions. Creswell (2009) defines quantitative research as the "means for testing objective theories by examining the relationship among variables" (p. 4). Quantitative studies use numbers rather than words and ask closed-ended versus open-ended questions used in qualitative studies (Creswell, 2009). Some researchers also conduct "mixed methods" studies that combine both quantitative and qualitative techniques in studying a single issue.

To put all of this in perspective, a descriptive study may provide data on how many teachers leave the profession each year. A more in-depth quantitative study could assess several variables to see whether, all else being equal, teachers in low-performing schools left at higher rates than teachers at high-performing schools or whether teachers with less experience are more likely to leave than those with more years of service. Qualitative researchers would likely interview some number of teachers—those who left and didn't leave—to understand the teachers' reasons for leaving, as perhaps there are variables not considered in the quantitative study. Or a qualitative researcher might shadow (study) a teacher over the course of a school year to observe his/her work environment and then might extrapolate hypotheses about why teachers might leave the profession based on the researcher's observations.

Whether qualitative or quantitative, scientific studies follow a similar organizational format. Most begin with an introduction of the problem including why study of the issue is relevant to policy, conditions, scholarship, and/or knowledge in general. This is followed by a review of the existing academic literature. What do we know about the topic and what is yet to be known? This often allows the author to show how his or her study will contribute to what is already known and provides some grounding for the study. A theoretical or conceptual framework provides a lens through which the author is focusing the study. It also helps in determining a hypothesis about what the author thinks the result(s) might be. The author then details his/her research methods to allow peers and readers to assess the rigor, trustworthiness, and validity of the study. Any academic studies involving interaction with people require approval by institutional review boards to ensure the physical and emotional safety of the research subjects. Studies utilizing personal data (e.g., student test scores) require compliance with federal and state privacy laws. By detailing research methods in the published study, readers can assess whether it appears that the author set up a proper research protocol and whether the author considered all potential variables or impacts. Following the methods section are the results of the study. In quantitative studies, there are many tables and charts depicting statistical results. Qualitative studies may also use charts and graphs, but they will mostly focus on themes stemming from the data accompanied by quotations from respondents (such as if interviews were used to gather data). Finally, the research paper will conclude with a discussion and implications section. This section allows the author to draw conclusions from the results and indicate how the results may impact policy, programs, and/or future research. The author may also acknowledge certain limitations of the study (e.g., limited availability of data) and then make suggestions for future research projects on the topic.

These studies are published in hundreds of academic education-related and other journals[1] that can be found through most brick-and-mortar and online university libraries. It is a bit more difficult for the average person to access these journals because most are subscription-based, which is one of the potential reasons research does not easily find its way to policymakers and staff. Public libraries sometimes host free public access to the more popular journals.

The Internet has allowed for the expansion of alternate channels of research development and publication. Some think tanks, associations, and advocacy groups conduct their own research projects and disseminate them freely through websites, webinars, and podcasts. Government agencies may also support an in-house research function or contract out specific studies to university-based or other researchers. More extensive discussion on the supply of research occurs later.

The previous section on types of research is but the tip of a very large iceberg. Multiple graduate courses are offered on research methods, and scholars often specialize in one type of research method. While those working with education policy do not necessarily need to be qualitative and/or quantitative research experts, it does help if such professionals understand how to read and interpret the research. This can only ensure that professionals are knowledgeable consumers who do not necessarily have to rely on third parties to gather and interpret findings. The Education Commission of the States offers a research primer for policymakers (noted in the "For Further Information" section) and is a good foundation to gain such knowledge.

Research Utilization

So far, this chapter has covered the difficulties inherent in connecting education research and policy, types of research, format of research articles, and where to find research. This next section will dive more deeply into how research is used by policymakers, including both the demand from policymakers for research and the supply of research from various organizations. Although this chapter will present studies specific to research utilization in the policy process, it is also important to remember the theories of the policy process presented in Chapter 3, as those also consider the relevance of research, or more broadly, information, in the policy process. For instance, the multiple streams theory suggests that the application of information to policy is not a linear process. Rather, parallel streams of problems, solutions, and politics continually flow, and when all three come together, assisted by an event or a policy entrepreneur, a policy item gets on the macro political and policy agenda (Kingdon, 2011). Information and research could be a part of any of those streams.

So, woven throughout this chapter is the notion that it may be unrealistic to assume that the demand and supply chain between policymakers and researchers will be perfectly efficient—that quality research is supplied and quickly applied to some pressing social ill. For starters, there is a lag time between identification of an education policy issue that needs to be addressed and the ability to produce quality research (Birnbaum, 2000). Once a policy issue is identified, there are no proverbial red phones sitting on researchers' desks to inform them of policymakers' research needs. When researchers do become aware of critical policy issues, time is needed to assess current knowledge of the problem, design the study, get permission from institutional review boards to conduct the study, carry out the research, analyze results, write the resulting report or article, and disseminate the material to appropriate audiences. Unfortunately, this lag time is sometimes seen as indifference or inefficiency on the part of researchers and universities. Cultural issues are also in play as the education policy, political, and research worlds are vastly different, even though both groups are working toward a similar goal—solving important educational issues. Ness (2010) summarizes researcher Jeffrey Henig's (2008, 2009) apt conception of the cultural differences between researchers and policymakers:

- Policymakers need timely answers to policy problems, but research often takes long periods of time.
- Policymakers look for a "silver bullet" answer to a problem, whereas researchers view existing knowledge cumulatively.
- Policymakers are moved to action by compelling facts, but researchers understand the complexities surrounding causality, which can make them somewhat hesitant to provide policy prescriptions.
- Policymakers prefer concrete evidence, whereas researchers are comfortable with abstract concepts, broad themes, and implications.
- Policymakers need to simplify concepts and communications, while researchers embrace nuances and complexity, usually in lengthy analyses.

Birnbaum (2000) notes that these cultural differences do not make one group better than the other:

> Policy scholars don't know *better* than policy makers; they just know *different* than policy makers. Policy scholars may reject propositions that deny the ground assumptions of their field; policy makers may reject propositions that deny their common sense. What is unusual and interesting to one group may be considered common and obvious to the other. The strength of scholars is that they are detached from the problems they study; they know that they must not be distracted by irrelevant details if they are to develop basic principles. The strength of policy makers is that they are completely absorbed by the problems with which they deal; they know that only those embedded in the daily chaos of seemingly irrelevant details can make sound judgments in a dynamic environment. . . . What is important is not that individual studies affect

individual decisions, but that scholarly work over time influences the systems of knowledge and belief that give meaning to policy.

(pp. 126–127)

Demand

Any conversation about research utilization should focus on both the demand and supply of research. Demand addresses policymakers' desires for and particular use of research. Does someone actually read and use the thousands (perhaps millions) of research articles, reports, books, and blogs on education policy topics? The previous section suggested that just because there is not a perfectly efficient direct application of research to policy problems does not mean that research does not influence policy. Ness (2010), relying heavily on Carol Weiss's work on the uses of research, describes three distinct types of research utilization. The first is *instrumental use.* This is what most people consider the ideal application. Research is conducted that can squarely inform a pressing policy or social problem. There is direct application of research to policy in the instrumental model. For example, a research study that determines a causal relationship between high school dropout rates and school size may incent new policy on school sizes. As cautioned previously, policymakers must carefully evaluate the context in which the research took place and whether the results would be likely in the current context. Instrumental use of research could also include studies on the costs, benefits, and potential implementation challenges of a certain policy (Hess, 2008).

The second is *conceptual use.* Conceptual application of research includes "the cumulative effect of a broad range of studies" (Ness, 2010, p. 9) that provides a general understanding of the field. Rather than a direct relationship to policy, research provides a foundation of knowledge that can be called upon when a problem rises to a policy agenda. Weiss (1979) cautions that while research can certainly be used conceptually to enlighten an issue, oversimplification and distortion can also "endarken" or confuse an issue. Again, proper understanding of research is important.

Finally, Ness (2010) suggests that research can be used *politically,* meaning that it is used in a tactical or symbolic manner. Weiss (1979) explains that a political research utilization model is one in which "partisans flourish the evidence in an attempt to neutralize opponents, convince waverers, and bolster supporters" (p. 429). Similar to the partisan approach, political use of research also includes tactical maneuvers that are less related to the actual substance of the research and used more to deal with thorny issues (Weiss, 1979). For instance, politicians and their staff may refer to ongoing research as evidence that a topic or issue is being addressed, or they may claim they are delaying action on an issue until the research is completed. They may also use research to deflect criticism by stating they relied on particular research studies in taking a certain course of action (Weiss, 1979).

Demand for educational research in policymaking has roots in *Brown v. Board of Education* (1954) and President Johnson's Great Society programs. However, the demand for educational research grew dramatically with the passage of the federal reauthorization of ESEA known as the No Child Left Behind Act of 2001. In fact, the term "scientifically based research" was mentioned 111 times in the law. This was a demand for a specific type of research meant to provide a stronger foundation for education policy programs. U.S. Department of Education officials stated that this type of research should replace commonly used alternatives to scientific research such as tradition, superstition, and anecdotes. The department's view of scientifically based research, which appears to continue today, moves more toward a medical model of research employing experimental techniques or other rigorous methods (U.S. Department of Education, 2002).

Studies conducted on the demand for research in developing policy are not numerous. However, there are a few that can enlighten this previous discussion on demand. In 2005, Hird published a study on state legislators' demand for research. Hird (2005) used a broad definition of research to encompass any relevant information and found that legislators' most important information sources when considering policy proposals were constituents. Second to constituents were the legislatures' own nonpartisan research organizations. Although these nonpartisan research organizations were not *influential* in ways such as analyzing information and providing new ideas to the legislature, they were *helpful* in gathering and summarizing information (Hird, 2005). Ness (2010) also notes that "researchers find that policymakers prefer 'insider' sources of information, such as legislative staff and fellow legislators to 'outsider' sources, such as the media and academics" (p. 12).

Supply

Supply has never been perfectly coupled with demand, but a rapidly grow-ing group of think tanks and other organizations that are now able to disseminate information through websites, portals, and blogs has certainly changed the supply landscape. Rigorous scientific research continues to be generated largely from institutions of higher education. At research-oriented institutions, a good portion of a faculty member's time and effort is dedicated to research. However, organizational incentives dictate that fac-ulty members work to publish their research in top-tier academic journals, usually ones that policymakers do not access. Because faculty members' tenure and promotion requirements center on these types of publications, research agendas may often be shaped by what is likely to be publishable rather than by what is needed to inform policy. Sometimes these two needs overlap, especially if, as noted previously, the policy need has been prominent long enough to give researchers an opportunity to design, con-duct, and publish research on the subject. For example, a flurry of recently published research articles on college completion and performance-based funding are directly relevant to current policymaking issues. Even still, it is incumbent on the faculty member or some other organization to publi-cize the study in a way that policymakers will find it, read it, and under-stand it. Unless a faculty member resides in a public research institution that has expectations of service to the state given its public nature, there really is no expectation to do this. Even in a public research university, greater incentives could be instituted and practices developed for dissemi-nating policy-relevant research more widely.

Beyond academic institutions, external groups, often called *intermediary organizations,* are influential in disseminating, and sometimes conducting, policy-relevant education research. External actors influencing education policy is not new. This began in the early 20th century with the emergence of Frederick Taylor's scientific management theories that focused chiefly on efficiency (Murnane & Willett, 2011). While first applied to business, the demands for greater efficiencies also became present in public affairs. Trujillo (2014) notes that

> from that point on, the bonds between external consultants from business and industry and school administrators were fixed. No longer were educators and communities left to their devices to deliberate about and solve their own problems; individual consultants or firms were regularly hired to collect data from the schools, pinpoint the errors in their ways to their leaders, and design reforms intended to tighten up the bureaucratic slack.
>
> (Cuban, 1988, p. 209)

This can be seen in the role of intermediary organizations today. Not only are consultants providing advice to schools, districts, and agencies, but intermediary organizations are "consulting" with policymakers by providing data, information, research, and policy proscriptions. In a sense, intermediary organizations dismantle the traditional "iron triangle" existing between government agencies, interest groups, and politicians, and this allows different actors to influence state and federal policy (Scott & Jabbar, 2014). We can still see Frederick Taylor's scientific management notions being played out in education today through K–12 accountability systems, college rating systems, value-added scores for teachers, and increasing use of data and predictive analytics.

There are three types of intermediary organizations. First, there are expert groups like the Education Commission of the States or the Southern Regional Education Board that strive to produce and disseminate information in a non-partisan and non-ideological manner. Second, membership groups such as the State Higher Education Executive Officers (SHEEO) and the Council of Chief State School Officers often have a research dissemination and/or production function largely tied to the association's aims and goals. Finally, there are ideological organizations that champion a particular cause or viewpoint, such as StudentsFirst, started by former District of Columbia chancellor Michelle Rhee, which focuses on teacher accountability reforms, and the Center for Education Reform, which advocates for expanded school choice options.

A recent study on the use of research and the role of intermediaries in New Orleans's K–12 reforms found that governmental organizations like the Recovery School District relied on local and national external brokers of information rather than in-house expertise given the lack of research capacity (DeBray, Scott, Lubienski, & Jabbar, 2014). The study did not note whether the Recovery School District strategically organized this way because they decided it was more efficient (monetarily or time-wise) to outsource that function. However, perhaps what is most troubling is that the researchers perceived a lack of internal technical capacity to evaluate the external research. For instance, users of the research evaluated it by "name brand" of the producing organization (e.g., Stanford University) or by "endorsements of trusted individuals in their policy networks" (DeBray et al., 2014, p. 202). The study also calls into question how governmental officials, in this case from the Recovery School District, used the obtained research, given that momentum on existing reforms accelerated even though the research questioned some components of the reforms (DeBray et al., 2014).

Another study examined the role of foundations in supporting education-related intermediary organizations. The authors found that the studied foundations acted as the hub of a wheel with their funded organizations as the spokes (Scott & Jabbar, 2014). Foundations established and/or sustained multiple organizations in order to generate coordinated movement on an advocacy platform. Foundations funded research by the intermediary organizations and helped them package and distribute the research to policymakers. The authors note,

> these findings show the critical importance of foundations not only for the organizational stability of national-level IOs, but also in terms of the kinds of reform issues taken up, the kinds of research that IOs engage in and promote, and the overall set of organizational priorities, . . . As the center of the wheel . . . foundations can be critical in determining which ideas or initiatives move ahead, which organizations are high quality and worthy of private and public investments, and which stall.
>
> (p. 244)

Therefore, foundation funded research must be carefully examined for adherence to proper research protocols to ensure it is a true research—rather than advocacy—piece.

In an examination of national and state K–12 education reform advocacy organizations, McGuinn (2012) found common elements among the groups, although they were not part of one coordinated effort. Most had a connection to school choice, particularly charter schools, and they advocated for improving teacher quality and intervening in chronically poor-performing schools. These organizations (including StudentsFirst, 50CAN, Stand for Children, and others) utilized both internal and external strategies to push their agendas. They held briefings for state policymakers where they reflected back state data and offered suggestions based on work in other states. They also disseminated information and mobilized citizens to demand educational reform. Some of these groups also raised funds to contribute to particular political races. McGuinn (2012) states, "this kind of hardball political organizing and lobbying has long been employed by the unions to defeat school reform legislation but increasingly is being utilized by the ERAOs [education reform advocacy organizations] to drive change" (p. 29).

Finally, a recent study examined the rising influence of ideologically based think tanks, another form of intermediary organization. Ness and Gandara (2014) found that politically conservative state-level think tanks are more prevalent than their progressive counterparts. All states had at least one state-level conservative think tank, while only 32 states had progressive think tanks. On average, both types of think tanks had similar-sized budgets. The conservative think tanks were more networked, often mentioning and cross-referencing other conservative think tanks on their websites. In relation to their higher education policy activity, which was the focus of the study, progressive and conservative think tanks held different priorities. The conservative think tanks were more likely to call for cuts to higher education funding and greater efficiencies, while progressive think tanks were more likely to call for greater state investments (Ness & Gandara, 2014).

A specific type of intermediary organization is the media. They have a unique role in presenting education-related information to the public, which includes policymakers and their constituents. Often, this is the only way that the general public receives information, including educational research results. Unfortunately, it appears that journalists rarely publicize educational research. In a study of 650 daily newspapers, the weekly K–12 newspaper *Education Week*, and online-only sites that focused on or wrote extensively on education over the first six months of 2010, the researcher found that only 0.69% of the education-related items that ran in the sampled outlets during the sampled days mentioned education research (Yettick, 2015). Only 3% of those items noting education research mentioned peer-reviewed journal research, but 45% of those items mentioned government-produced research. Interestingly, when specifically examining online-only outlets with university sponsors, less than 5% of items mentioned peer-reviewed research, about the same as with the general media (Yettick, 2015). One would think universities would highlight their faculties' own research. Other findings include university research (not necessarily cited as peer reviewed) and think tank research being cited at the same rates. The overwhelming majority of think tank mentions were advocacy-oriented rather than those that have a more neutral or academic approach (Yettick, 2015).

Yettick (2015) supplemented her analytic study with interviews of journalists. The top reasons for failure to cite or include peer-reviewed education research in articles was difficulty in understanding the research and the amount of time needed to find and review the research. Cost in accessing the research was another barrier.

The results of this study are rather disheartening given the role media outlets could have in disseminating education research and information. When the media does address an issue of educational importance,

> journalists all too often conjure up controversy where it does not exist, focus on the personalities of the parties involved, look to vested interest groups for commentary, and give equal time and attention to two sides of an issue even when the preponderance of evidence suggests that only one is right.
>
> (Howell, 2008, p. 139)

Conclusion

There is no shortage of education-related research to be used in designing, implementing, and assessing policy. The trick is to ensure that relevant people (policymakers, staff, media) know about it, are able to access it, and can understand it. This requires innovation from both researchers and users.

If university structures continue to incentivize the publication of research in academic journals, researchers may need a systematic way to repackage and deliver policy-relevant research results to appropriate audiences. Perhaps university departments, colleges, and/or centers could have dedicated professionals experienced in translating research for lay audiences and identifying appropriate communication channels.

Policymakers and other audiences need to be more informed consumers of research. This includes understanding the difference between descriptive data, correlations, and causality. It also includes being able to critically evaluate context if a policymaker is tempted to replicate a program or policy featured in a study. Finally, it includes taking note of who produced the research, given the rise of intermediary organizations. Is the researcher and/or funder of the research neutral to the research topic? Is the information presented truly research, or is this an information/advocacy brief? Consideration of these factors should help bridge the so-called divide between researchers and policymakers and facilitate thoughtful application of research to policy.

For Further Information

- The American Education Research Association (AERA) is the largest association of education researchers; they study early childhood education through adult learning issues: www.aera.net
- The Education Resources Information Center (ERIC) is a clearinghouse of education research that has been administered by the U.S. Department of Education's Institute of Education Sciences since 1964: http://eric.ed.gov
- The National Center for Education Statistics (NCES) houses an extremely large database of information, tables, and figures on early learning through higher education topics: http://nces.ed.gov
- The Directory of Open Access Journals indexes and provides access to some open access and peer-reviewed academic journals: https://doaj.org
- The Education Commission of the States hosts an online resource, "A Policymaker's Primer on Education Research," that assists policymakers and others in understanding, evaluating, and using research: www.ecs.org/html/educationissues/research/primer/aboutprimer.asp

- *Public Policy in an Uncertain World* by Charles F. Manski (2013) provides a critical look at using research to develop public policy.

Note

1. Those interested in education research are also advised to review public administration, political science, organizational theory, history, and psychology/child development journals for relevant education-related research.

References

Birnbaum, R. (2000). Policy scholars are from Venus; Policy makers are from Mars. *The Review of Higher Education, 23* (2), pp.119–132.

Brown v. Board of Education of Topeka, 347 U.S. 483 (1954).

Creswell, J. (2009). *Research design—Qualitative, quantitative, and mixed method approaches* (3rd ed.). Thousand Oaks, CA: Sage.

Cuban, L. (1988). *The managerial imperative and the practice of leadership in schools.* Albany: State University of New York Press.

DeBray, E., Scott, J., Lubienski, C., & Jabbar, H. (2014). Intermediary organizations in charter school policy coalitions: Evidence from New Orleans. *Educational Policy, 28*(2), 175–206.

Henig, J. (2008). The evolving relationship between researchers and public policy. In F. M. Hess (Ed.), *When research matters: How scholarship influences education policy* (pp. 41–62). Cambridge, MA: Harvard Education Press.

Henig, J. (2009). Politicization of evidence: Lessons for an informed democracy. *Educational Policy, 23*(1), 137–160.

Hess, F. (2008). *When research matters: How scholarship influences education policy.* Cambridge, MA: Harvard University Press.

Hird, J. (2005). Policy analysis for what? The effectiveness of nonpartisan policy research organizations. *The Policy Studies Journal, 33*(1), 83–105.

Howell, W. (2008). Education policy, academic research, and public opinion. In F. Hess (Ed.), *When research matters: How scholarship influences education policy* (pp. 135–154). Harvard Education Press: Cambridge, MA.

Kingdon, J. (2011). *Agendas, Alternatives, and Public Policies* 2nd Ed. Boston, MA: Longman.

Lubienski, C., Scott, J., & DeBray, E. (2014). The politics of research production, promotion, and utilization in educational policy. *Educational Policy, 28*(2), 131–144.

Manski, C. (2013). *Public Policy in an Uncertain World: Analysis and Decisions.* Cambridge, MA: Harvard University Press.

McGuinn, P. (2012, Summer). Fight club: Are advocacy organizations changing the politics of education? *Education Next*, 25–31.

Merriam, S. (2009). *Qualitative research: A guide to design and implementation.* San Francisco, CA: Jossey-Bass.

Murnane, R., & Willett, J. (2011). *Methods matter: Improving causal inference in educational and social science research.* New York, NY: Oxford Press.

Ness, E. (2010). The role of information in the policy process: Implications for the examination of research utilization in higher education policy. In J. C. Smart (Ed.), *Higher education: Handbook of theory and research* (pp. 1–49). Springer: New York.

Ness, E., & Gandara, D. (2014). Ideological think tanks in the states: An inventory of their prevalence, networks, and higher education policy activity. *Educational Policy, 28*(2), 258–280.

Scott, J., & Jabbar, H. (2014). The hub and the spokes: Foundations, intermediary organizations, incentivist reforms, and the politics of research evidence. *Educational Policy, 28*(2), 233–257.

Trujillo, T. (2014). The modern cult of efficiency: Intermediary organizations, incentivist reforms, and the politics of research evidence. *Educational Policy, 28*(2), 207–232.

U.S. Department of Education. (2002, February 6). *Scientifically based research.* Retrieved from www2.ed.gov/nclb/methods/whatworks/research/index.html

Weiss, C. (1979). The many meanings of research utilization. *Public Administration Review, 39*(5), 426–431.

Yettick, H. (2015). One small droplet: News media coverage of peer-reviewed and university-based education research and academic expertise. *Educational Researcher, 44*(3), 173–184.

Chapter 8

The Promise of P–20 Collaboration

The premise of this book is that those wanting to study, research, or work in education policy must have some knowledge of the entire pipeline if greater educational attainment is the nation's and states' collective goal. Basic knowledge of how the pipeline works, as presented in this book, is a good start. Perhaps consistent and effective collaboration between the educational sectors is also needed. Connections between the sectors become especially important given the changes in American education over the last century. It was only about 100 years ago that secondary schooling through grade 12 became widespread. In the later part of the 20th century, America began a move toward mass higher education with the implementation of the GI Bill. Mass higher education is increasing with current calls for all students to be prepared for some type of postsecondary education. Public early learning options such as pre-kindergarten are becoming more widespread as well. The typical educational experience is no longer just kindergarten through 12th grade. Greater percentages of American students are participating in all three sectors of education: early learning, K–12, and higher education. This requires the sectors—at national, state, and local levels—to coordinate policies to ensure students move efficiently and effectively through the entire educational system. Random acts of access and success will not address what are increasingly becoming systemic issues of connection.

For example, there is a key pipeline transition point from high school graduation to college entry that raises a host of connection questions such as:

- Is there a culture that sets the expectation for students to attend postsecondary education?
- Do students have the information needed to make decisions about postsecondary education such as where to go, how to pay, and how to enroll?
- Are students academically prepared for college entry?
- Are institutions of higher education prepared for greater numbers of and more diverse students?

Several statewide policies and practices can affect this transition point, including:

- Ensuring alignment between statewide high school graduation requirements and basic college entry requirements
- Alignment of high school curriculums with introductory college courses
- Sharing of the same information between high school counselors and postsecondary financial and admissions counselors
- Providing ample, accessible, and timely information about postsecondary education to students and parents.

Typically, these policies and practices involve several state agencies, such as the state department of education, the state higher education agency, a technical college system (if separate from the higher education agency), a student finance agency, and perhaps others. If more students are going to traverse the sectors, which involves several governmental agencies, it seems to be common sense that there should be greater communication and collaboration between those agencies. This concluding chapter will examine various collaborative efforts and the evidence of their impact on educational outcomes and efficiency.

The Need for Collaboration

Michael Kirst, professor emeritus at Stanford University and president of the California State Board of Education, has perhaps been the most vocal in arguing that the broken pipeline between K–12 and higher education harms postsecondary access and success. He notes that students, rather than policies, are the primary connection between the two sectors (Kirst & Venezia, 2003). While this may make sense on its face, a system connected only by student matriculation is connected by millions of individual tiny, fragile threads dependent on the ability of the student/family to make connections rather than a solid, wide pipeline that facilitates movement. For example, whether a student attends college can depend on whether a family receives adequate information about college, and provision of this information is not always available to all students equally. In a study conducted by Stanford's Bridge Project, Kirst and Venezia (2003) found that

> Forty-two percent, 44 percent, and 47 percent of economically disadvantaged parents in Illinois, Maryland, and Oregon, respectively, stated that they had received college information, as compared with 74 percent, 71 percent, and 66 percent of their more economically well-off counterparts.

Kirst and Venezia's Bridge Project conducted another study that found "88 percent of all high school students surveyed—and over 80 percent of African American and Hispanic high school students—said they plan to attend some form of postsecondary education" (Kirst and Venezia, 2003). In reality, as of 2013, only 66% of all high school completers immediately enrolled in postsecondary education. Percentages are lower for Black high school graduates (57%) and Hispanic graduates (60%) (National Center for Education Statistics, 2015). Not only do we need greater numbers and percentages of students going to college, we need them to be prepared for college. Yet, there is

> evidence that the wide chasm between K–12 and higher education is . . . a major contributor to poor student preparation for college . . . [and] is particularly disastrous for students of color and students from low-income families.
>
> (Kirst & Venezia, 2003)

Kirst and Venezia are not the only ones arguing for greater connections between education sectors. Researcher Burton Clark was presenting evidence of the disjuncture 30 years ago. Clark used international comparisons to demonstrate that our inherited system of education represented by fragmented governance and sectors is not the only way. He found that Americans take for granted the alignment between elementary and secondary schools into one K–12 system. "Common administrative frameworks tend to pull secondary education toward the elementary school rather than towards the university. This is so natural a part of the U.S. educational system that it is rarely even considered, much less questioned" (Clark, 1985, p. 394). Some other developed countries view high school as preparation for college, not an end in itself. Sometimes students only get one chance to perform well on a high school exam that determines their future educational paths. America seems to value opportunities for second chances and educational attainment well into adulthood, which creates a winding rather than a perfectly straight pipeline. Clark also notes that some other countries do not utilize local school boards and instead administer public schools nationally or through regional clusters, which could also help create uniform policies and structures that facilitate movement through the pipeline (Clark, 1985).

Today, education leaders recognize the need for greater connections between the sectors. A recent survey of K–12 and higher education leaders found that 90% of K–12 respondents and 80% of higher education respondents believe collaboration with the other sector is important. On the other hand, only one-third of respondents believe that currently existing collaborations are effective (edBridge Partners & Hart Research Associates, 2014). Much of the existing research on the need for education collaboration focuses on the important transition between K–12 and higher education. There is not as much concerning the connections between early learning and K–12 given the recent movement to more widespread public systems of early learning. However, the discussion here concerning collaboration is entirely relevant to all transition points in the pipeline.

While the federal government can and does use its national platform and provisions of funding to address educational attainment and pipeline issues, education remains under the sole authority of states. Therefore, this section will focus on collaboration between P–20 agencies at the state level.

Public administration and organizational researchers have studied public agency collaboration extensively. It is interesting that we are just now considering education sector collaboration and working to apply this knowledge. To be clear, the relevant definition of cross-sector collaboration here is "the linking or sharing of information, resources, activities, and capabilities by organizations in two or more sectors to achieve jointly an outcome that could not be achieved by organizations in one sector separately" (Bryson, Crosby, & Stone, 2006, p. 44). What this literature makes clear is that cross-sector collaboration is difficult. It is not as simple as scheduling a meeting, inviting the collaborators, and waiting for good things to happen. Agency leaders have their own work. For example, the early learning commissioner is charged with administering early childhood programs, and it is probably unlikely that an explicit part of his or her job description is collaborating with K–12. Only when agency leaders see the value in collaboration and perhaps the benefit to their individual work will collaboration be imperative. "Public policy makers are most likely to try cross-sector collaboration when they believe the separate efforts of different sectors to address a public problem have failed or are likely to fail, and the actual or potential failures cannot be fixed by the sectors acting alone" (Bryson et al., 2006, p. 46). At the macro level, perhaps the inability to rapidly increase the educational attainment rate is the failure. Or perhaps at a more micro level, it is low third grade reading proficiency or high college remediation rates. However wide or narrow we make the picture, it seems that education agencies, on their own, have not been able to significantly move the needle on these and other metrics. Perhaps collaboration can help.

Barriers to Collaboration

First, it is important to acknowledge the very real barriers to collaboration. As noted previously, agencies have their "day job" so to speak, but there are other issues that may make expenditure of energy and resources on collaborating difficult. At a very basic level, the state education governance structure is one issue. As discussed more in depth in Chapter 2, states have developed myriad configurations for administration of early childhood through postsecondary education. This usually includes some combination of state boards and administrative agencies to set broad goals, develop policies, and manage program delivery for each sector of P–20 education. Separate administrative agencies and legislative committees create uncoordinated budgets, laws, and rules for early childhood, K–12, and higher education that foster separate constituencies, interest groups, and cultures. In short, the system was designed in a disjointed manner. Public administration researchers have analyzed the barriers to collaboration between public agencies. Whetten and Bozeman (1991) developed a list of six potential barriers to interagency collaboration in the public sector:

1. *Mission barriers.* These occur when organizational missions overlap or are in conflict. For example, in a state with both a university system and a technical college system, both have a mission to provide higher education for the state's citizens, but which entity provides which degree programs and where? Case studies of state P–20 councils have shown that mission barriers do indeed occur. As one P–20 council member stated, "The barriers are sort of obvious. In some way you have natural barriers . . . when you have different organizations that are run for different purposes or have different responsibilities" (Rippner, 2015, p. 28)

2. *Political barriers.* These occur when agencies report to or have loyalty to different politicians or state leaders. A K–12 chief state school officer elected by the state's citizens has a different loyalty than other education agency leaders who may be appointed by the governor or a state board.

3. *Resource barriers.* Agency competition for scarce state resources can be a barrier to open and effective collaboration. Leaders may not want to share resources or may want to try to solve problems on their own in order to gain more resources. Further, lack of resources to support the collaboration may prevent success.

4. *Legal barriers.* A constitutionally fragmented government erects legal barriers to collaboration. Any state education governance configuration that is not completely directed by the governor may result in legal barriers to collaboration.

5. *Constituent barriers.* Overlapping constituencies, conflict between constituencies, or agency cooptation by constituencies may present barriers. If an agency feels beholden to a constituency and that presents conflict with constituencies of other agencies, issues arise. For instance, a state schools superintendent may have difficulty collaborating on a statewide dual enrollment policy intended to increase postsecondary access and

success if one of his/her constituencies—local school superintendents—fears losing funding for students from their enrollment in postsecondary institutions.

6. *Bureaucratic barriers.* Sometimes the good things about bureaucracies, such as specialized knowledge and routines, can hinder innovation through collaboration as staff protect a traditional way of doing things. Also, sometimes the knowledge needed to address an issue is stored at lower levels of an agency and is not at the collaboration table.

Given this knowledge of potential barriers, states have a better chance to avoid or address them in attempting collaborative efforts. First, it helps to understand what states have attempted thus far.

Methods of Collaboration

One method of promoting a more seamless state education system is through integrated governance structures. New York, Idaho, and Pennsylvania have long had integrated governance structures that utilize the same governing board and/or agency to administer two or more educational sectors. In 2000, Florida was the first state in the last several decades to reform its traditional, fragmented state structure and adopt a unified education governance system with early childhood education through higher education governed by a single board and administered through one agency (although this has changed a bit since then). The legislative purpose of the restructuring was to promote enhanced student achievement, resource efficiency, seamlessness, and consistency (Florida Education Governance Reorganization Act, 2000). Two additional states, Oregon and Rhode Island, have also recently enacted state education governance changes in furtherance of a consolidated P–20 structure (Smith & Fulton, 2013).

For those states without an integrated structure, a P–20 council may help with collaboration. A state P–20 council may take many forms, but it generally includes representatives from different education sectors such as early childhood education, K–12, and higher education. The *P* represents pre-kindergarten and the *20* represents education through graduate school. These councils can also be referred to as P–16, K–16, or K–20 councils, depending on the education sectors represented on the council.

There are 22 active state P–20 councils in the U.S. (Rippner, 2014), and their characteristics vary greatly. First, membership size ranges from as few as 7 members to as many as 50. This is because some councils restrict membership to state agency leaders, whereas others include business and community members, educators, and legislators. The governor or a representative is often a member and/or chairman of the council. Governors also appoint some or all P–20 council members in the vast majority of states. Councils vary by meeting frequency, the availability of staff support, and monetary resources. Most councils address such issues as high school to college transitions; integrated data systems; K–12 teacher development; postsecondary retention, transfer, and completion; and early learning (Dounay, 2009).

P–20 councils are often created, transformed, or dismantled with a change in gubernatorial leadership. Since 2008, when there were 38 P–20 councils (ECS, 2013), 3 states transitioned from using P–20 councils to developing more integrated state governance structures, 16 states disbanded their P–20 councils, and 13 states transformed their councils in some way (Rippner, 2014). For example, Illinois has conducted P–20 collaborations since the late 1990s, and the form of these has changed over the years. Research found that early collaborative efforts were not as effective as desired:

> From one K–12 respondent's perspective . . . the joint education committee is 'a wonderful idea without authority, a very ineffective group' where meetings exemplify the gulf [between K–12 and higher education]. 'They sit on one side, we sit on the other'.
> (Richardson, Bracco, Callan, & Finney, 1999, p. 165)

Illinois subsequently retooled the structure of its council in the late 2000s and is seeing improved results (Rippner, 2014).

P–20 Council Performance

Staying focused on P–20 councils, since most states have utilized one over the past several years and they are relatively easier to initiate than a whole-scale governance structure change, it is important to present their benefits and drawbacks. Again, this emphasis on P–20 councils assumes that collaboration between state education sectors would produce more coherent education policies that facilitate greater educational achievement and attainment.

First, there are many potential benefits of P–20 councils. They can build consensus among relevant actors, provide a venue for regular discussion of cross-cutting issues, ensure that decision making is centered on students rather than a particular organization, promote efficiency through elimination of redundancies in service, and enhance the tax base through a more educated (and higher paid) population (Dounay, 2009). Many of these benefits could be attributed to collaboration in general rather than specifically through a P–20 council, but the council does provide the venue from which regular collaboration can take place. Most research on P–20 councils has found that councils improve relationships among education policy leaders through building trust and promoting regular communication between members (Davis & Hoffman, 2008; Lopez, 2010; Nunez & Oliva, 2009; Rippner, 2014). Recent research demonstrates that this helps to break down silos within and among agencies. In a comparative case study of P–20 councils, all three of the state councils studied attributed their progress on creation of a statewide longitudinal data system to the P–20 council (Rippner, 2014). Research has also shown that P–20 councils can help overcome state education structural barriers to collaboration, as discussed previously (Rippner, 2015).

On the other hand, there are few concrete outcomes stemming from P–20 councils. Stronger relationships are good, but how do they affect students? In part, this reflects the difficulty in defining a P–20 council's effectiveness. For example, attributing improved student achievement and/or attainment outcomes to the council's work is nefarious given the plethora of other variables and policies that may affect those outcomes. If student outcomes are set aside, then what else could P–20 councils be judged on? Some researchers look for concrete policies and/or programs developed and implemented by the councils. On this measure, P–20 councils are rather lackluster. Finney, Perna, and Callan (2014) note that while P–20 councils "raise awareness and encourage dialogue across state education sectors, they have had little success enacting policies to improve performance" (p. 8). Perna and Armijo (2014) agree: "P–20 councils have had minimal success . . . in establishing or changing public policies to create a more integrated educational system"

(p. 24). It does not appear that this is for lack of trying on the councils' part. Other researchers found that P–20 councils often engage in a good deal of discussion and planning, but falter when it comes to action (Rippner, 2014; Shulock, 2009). There are a few possible reasons for this. First, joint education policy ventures are difficult. If the education issues that P–20 councils are facing were easy, they would have been solved a long time ago. Closing achievement gaps between subgroups, ensuring all third graders read proficiently, and placing a quality teacher in every classroom are just examples of the thorny issues before these councils. Further, members of P–20 councils come with their own sets of goals, mandates, and resources that affect their approaches to solving these issues. Second, collaboration inertia may set it. This occurs when "the output from a collaborative arrangement is negligible, the rate of output is extremely slow, or stories of pain and hard grind are integral to success achieved" (Huxham & Vangen, 2004, p. 191). Inertia may set in when the group cannot agree on aims and/or members have hidden aims; issues of power arise; there is a lack of trust among group members; members are fatigued from too many collaborative ventures; or ambiguity, complexity, or change make it hard to grab hold of an issue to collaborate on (Huxham & Vangen, 2004). Prior research on P–20 councils has found all of these factors plaguing councils across the nation. This may be why some councils continue on, but engage in a merely symbolic form of planning. This concept was developed by Cohen and March (1974) and occurs when participants in the collaboration settle for the illusion of progress through the symbolic act of meeting/planning. A meeting was called, participants were there, a discussion ensued, and the work is done. Anecdotally, many P–20 council participants complain that collaboration can often settle into this type of "meet and greet" or "dog and pony show" pattern.

Going Forward

As one state higher education leader remarked:

> The concept of collaboration is one of those ideas that is sort of like motherhood. Surely you want to do it and should do it and there should be positive outcomes from collaboration. . . . I think the public expects

and wants state agencies to work together to a common good, so it's something we ought to do. It doesn't mean it's going to be successful.

(Rippner, 2014, p. 31)

Potential exists for more effective P–20 councils. However, merely deciding to collaborate is not enough to produce results. Attention must be given to the form and function of the council (Rippner, 2014). This must be specific to the state context in which the council sits, given the variety of political, historical, and policy contexts among states. For example, in one state it may be important to include legislators on the P–20 council because the state legislature is very influential and has a professionalized staff that can help legislators dive deeply into issues. Another state may choose to only include state agency leaders because previous attempts at collaboration included too many voices and traction was never made. Regardless of the composition of the P–20 council, the ideal role for members is to "recommend policy changes, influence legislatures and K–12 and postsecondary governing bodies in enacting these changes, and for council members in positions of authority to see that policy changes are implemented" (Dounay, 2008, p. 4). A member of one recently studied state council agreed: "We only wanted people who were responsible and accountable for getting something done as opposed to people who could inform us" (Rippner, 2015, p. 16).

Strong council leadership is also imperative. There must be someone holding the council accountable for results. This could be the governor, the legislature, or the chairman of the council. Illinois's P–20 council is held accountable by a former state legislator who was appointed chairman by the governor. A member of the council described the chairman as someone who "doesn't take any crap, so if he asks someone to do something he pretty much expects them to do it or explain why they're not doing it" (Rippner, 2015, p. 25). A leader needs to encourage the council to keep going, even through the complexities, and to maintain focus on agenda items that individual agencies could not accomplish alone.

Resources are also essential for an effective P–20 council (Rippner, 2014; Venezia, Callan, Finney, Kirst, & Usdan, 2005). Resources namely come in two forms: staff support and funding for joint projects. Professional support for a P–20 council can manage projects, encourage collaboration at lower levels of participating agencies, connect business or community resources as necessary, and keep track of progress toward goals. As one P–20 council member states, "stuff doesn't happen just because you hold the meeting. It's because of what happens in between those [meetings]" (Rippner, 2015, p. 26). Professional staff also provide a level of sustainability as council chairs and/or members change. There is great variation in P–20 council staffing structures. Hawaii's P–20 council boasts almost 30 staff members, and they manage a number of grants that overlap K–12 and higher education. Georgia's council utilizes one half-time professional staff member. Minnesota's council has no dedicated staff, but instead relies on "borrowed" staff from the chair's agency.

Finally, a culture of collaboration must be created. This encompasses a couple of components. First, a culture of collaboration transcends the unique cultures of early learning, K–12, and higher education. Each sector has its own general cultural components. For example, the traditions of faculty autonomy and governance are strong in higher education, but these do not really exist in early learning or K–12. Teacher accountability for student success is strong in K–12, but not in higher education. A P–20 council must establish a distinct culture that focuses on moving students successfully through the system rather than focusing on what can or cannot be done in existing sector cultures. It may be easier to develop and maintain this distinct culture at the collaboration table than to ensure it filters down through state educational institutions. Second, a culture of collaboration can be jump-started through "quick wins" (Bryson et al., 2006). Many councils initially attempt to tackle the biggest, thorniest, and likely most important education issues facing the state, such as how to decrease the high school dropout rate or how to meet the state's college completion goal. These are good organizing and guiding principles and goals, but they may cause frustration and collaboration inertia if they are the only concrete goals the council is working toward, given their complexity and elusiveness. Rather, councils should break down goals into more manageable actions and steps. For instance, perhaps ensuring curricular alignment between advanced placement science courses and introductory college science courses would be a good first step in increasing successful transitions between high school and college for science-interested students. An effective first step and early win will depend on the state's context and the council's charge.

Long-term, P–20 councils may do well to assess themselves against the following criterion of effective councils:

- The council identifies breaks in the P–20 pipeline and the reasons for such breaks.
- The council comes to consensus on potential solutions to remedy the breaks.
- An actionable plan is developed through policy, programs, and/or law to address the breaks.
- The council develops benchmarks to measure improvement.
- Leaders and the public understand the need for the council and come to expect alignment through communications of the council's work and successes.
- The council has the ability to work with other related stakeholders, such as interest groups, reform commissions, and business organizations (Dounay, 2010).

There are three areas where P–20 councils could potentially make a big state impact. These include alignment between high school graduation and college entry requirements, accountability, and data analysis.

Forty-seven states have minimum high school graduation requirements, yet only six states have completely aligned high school graduation requirements and higher education admissions policies. Twelve additional states have aligned coursework, but not for foreign language requirements (Glancy, Fulton, Anderson, Zinth, & Millard, 2014). This alignment is important to negate any type of purgatory between high school and college caused by a student believing that a high school diploma qualifies him/her for college entry, but finds him-/herself locked out of certain options. Achieve, Inc. and other education groups have long advocated for and encouraged states to undertake alignment work, but progress is slow.

P–20 councils could also develop and support a more integrated form of accountability. As states move to more rigorous college- and career-ready high school learning standards (as discussed in previous chapters), more students will hopefully be matriculating to some form of postsecondary education. Enhanced state data systems can help track individual students throughout the system, which creates the potential for a longitudinal accountability system. For example, as states begin holding high schools accountable for producing college- and career-ready students, focus will turn to how institutions of higher education serve those students. Are postsecondary institutions ready for more students? Are they ready for more prepared students? Longitudinal data systems should be able to assess whether there are breaks in the system, such as whether highly prepared high school graduates are performing poorly in their freshman year at certain colleges or whether highly prepared students from certain high schools are not matriculating to top colleges even though they are highly qualified. The possibility of integrated accountability may affect the traditional culture of higher education because

> while both fields have faced similar calls for assessment and evidence of results, the degree of professional control over this process is much greater in higher education than in K–12; and that higher education has been much more protected (thus far) from state and federal accountability pressures because of its reputation, its greater degree of professionalization, its market success, and the belief among policy makers that the key to higher education's success is its decentralized professional autonomy.
>
> (Mehta, 2014, p. 883)

P–20 councils can help create a "third culture" that is distinct from, but still respectful of, the existing cultures of K–12 and higher education that allow states to take a larger view of the educational system.

This chapter has focused on collaboration at the state level because this is where most education policies are created. However, local P–20 collaborative efforts exist and often focus on specific problems, issues, activities, and policies between a handful of institutions. Several localities support P–20 councils. Notably, Stark County, Ohio, operates an extensive collaborative network based on a foundation of research that such collaboration can help educational improvement. Some California school districts also operate P–20 councils. An interesting quantitative study on whether collaboration between K–12 and higher education through these local California councils affects high school graduation, college preparation, and college-going rates found that specific, noncomprehensive partnerships had no significant effect on any of the indicators (Domina & Ruzek, 2012). The noncomprehensive partnerships focused on only one or two specific initiatives. However, comprehensive partnerships had a significant effect over time on the percentage of ninth graders graduating high school and the percent enrolling in community colleges and the California State University system. There was no effect on the percentage completing a college preparatory program or enrolling in the elite University of California system (Domina & Ruzek, 2012).

At a local level, collaboration also happens between individual institutions of higher education and schools. This dates back over 100 years to when John Dewey initiated a laboratory K–12 school sponsored by the University of Chicago. These schools, which continue today in various states, allow for a close partnership between a college or department of education and a primary and/or secondary school; such partnerships foster hands-on training for novice teachers and the ability to conduct and apply educational research at the laboratory school. Institutions of higher education have also entered the charter schools field, with 46 colleges or universities across the nation chartering one or more schools.

Conclusion

This chapter has diverged somewhat from the others in that it is presenting information with the aim of making a case for collaboration between the education sectors. Previous chapters laid a foundation of knowledge about the history and structure of the U.S. educational system as well as specific details and trends in early childhood education, K–12, and higher education policy. Acknowledging the current state of the nation's educational achievement and attainment and examining the disjuncture between the sectors leads some thinkers, including the author, to consider whether a more seamless system might produce better and more efficient results.

There are myriad ways to work toward a more seamless system. One way is simply ensuring that those who are making and implementing educational policies have basic knowledge of the entire pipeline—hence, the goal of this book. This concluding chapter focused on a more actionable method of promoting seamlessness—state P–20 councils. These councils are in use in almost half of the states and are a relatively low-cost, low-burden way of forging collaboration (compared to whole-scale governance change). These councils are not without their issues, and mixed success to date requires renewed optimism and additional research into how to increase their effectiveness.

For Further Reading

- The Education Commission of the States website has a page dedicated to P–16 issues: www.ecs.org/html/issue.asp?issueID=76
- The Stanford University Bridge Project has undertaken a good amount of research on P–20 issues: http://web.stanford.edu/group/bridgeproject/
- The Stark County, Ohio, P–16 Compact is a strong example of a local P–16 council, and their website contains many resources for P–20 councils: www.edpartner.org/

References

Bryson, J., Crosby, B., & Stone, M. (2006, December). The design and implementation of cross-sector collaborations: Propositions from the literature. *Public Administration Review*, 44–55.

Clark, B. (1985, February). The high school and the university: What went wrong in America, Part 1. *Phi Delta Kappan*, 391–397.

Cohen, M., & March, J. (1974). *Leadership and ambiguity: The American college president*. Hightstown, NJ: McGraw-Hill.

Davis, R., & Hoffman, J. (2008). Higher education and the P–16 movement: What is to be done? *Thought & Action*, 123–134.

Domina, T., & Ruzek, E. (2012). Paving the way: K–16 partnerships for higher education diversity and high school reform. *Educational Policy, 26*, 243–267.

Dounay, J. (2008, November). *Landmines P–16/P–20 councils encounter—and how they can be addressed (or avoided altogether)*. Retrieved from www.ecs.org/html/Document.asp?chouseid=7886

Dounay, J. (2009, July 19). *P–20: A national perspective and keys to success*. Presentation from the Education Commission of the States Annual Conference, Nashville, TN.

Dounay, J. (2010, December 15). *What defines success for a P-20 council?* Retrieved from http://p-20matters.blogspot.com/2010/12/what-defines-success-for-p-20-council.html

edBridge Partners & Hart Research Associates. (2014, January). *The collabora-tion imperative—Findings from a survey of school district and post-secondary leaders*. Retrieved from www.edbridgepartners.com/research/?research=our-survey

Education Commission of the States (ECS). (2013, June). *P-16/P-20 database*. Retrieved from www.ecs.org

Finney, J., Perna, L., & Callan, P. (2014). *Renewing the promise: State policies to improve higher education performance*. Philadelphia: Institute for Research on Higher Edu-cation, University of Pennsylvania Graduate School of Education.

Florida Education Governance Reorganization Act, HB 2263, (2000).

Glancy, E., Fulton, M., Anderson, L., Zinth, J., & Millard, M. (2014, October). *Blueprint for college readiness: A 50-state policy analysis*. Retrieved from www.ecs. org/docs/ECSBlueprint.pdf

Huxham, C., & Vangen, S. (2004). Doing things collaboratively: Realizing the advantage or succumbing to inertia? *Organizational Dynamics, 33*(2), 190–201.

Kirst, M., & Venezia, A. (2003, Spring). Undermining student aspirations. *National Crosstalk*. Retrieved from www.highereducation.org/crosstalk/ct0203/voices0 203-undermining.shtml

Lopez, J. (2010). *Colorado's P-20 education coordinating council: 2007–2010*. Retrieved from http://cospl.coalliance.org/fedora/repository/co:8443

Mehta, J. (2014). When professions shape politics: The case of accountability in K–12 and higher education. *Educational Policy, 28*(6), 881–915.

National Center for Education Statistics. (2015). *Digest of education statistics*. Retrieved from www.nces.ed.gov

Nunez, A., & Oliva, M. (2009). Organizational collaboration to promote college access: A P-20 framework. *Journal of Hispanic Higher Education, 8*, 322–339.

Perna, L., & Armijo, M. (2014). The persistence of unaligned K–12 and higher education systems: Why have statewide alignment efforts been ineffective? *The ANNALS of the American Academy of Political and Social Science, 655*(16), 16–35.

Richardson, R., Bracco, K., Callan, P., & Finney, J., (1999). *Designing state higher education systems for a new century*. Phoenix, AZ: American Council on Education Oryx Press.

Rippner, J. (2014). State P-20 councils and collaboration between K-12 and higher education. *Educational Policy*. Advance online publication. doi:10.1177/ 0895904814558008

Rippner, J. (2015). Barriers to Success? The Role of Statewide Education Gover-nance Structures in P-20 Council Collaboration. *Education Policy Analysis Archives, 23*(76). Retrieved August 10, 2015, from http://epaa.asu.edu/ojs/article/ view/1909

Shulock, N. (2009). From dialogue to policy? A comparison of P–16 councils in three states. In The National Center for Public Policy and Higher Education (Ed.), *States, schools, and colleges: Policies to improve student readiness for college and strengthen coordination between schools and colleges* (pp. 133–139). The National Center for Public Policy and Higher Education, Washington, DC.

Smith, M., & Fulton, M. (2013, September). *Recent changes to postsecondary governance in states: 2011–13.* Retrieved from www.ecs.org/clearinghouse/01/09/33/10933.pdf

Venezia, A., Callan, P., Finney, J., Kirst, M., & Usdan, M. (2005). *The governance divide: A report on a four-state case study on improving college readiness and success.* San Jose, CA: The Institute for Educational Leadership, The National Center for Public Policy and Higher Education, The Stanford Institute for Higher Education Research.

Whetten, D. A., & Bozeman, B. (1991). Policy Coordination and Interorganizational Relations: Some Guidelines for Sharing Power. In J. M. Bryson, & R. C. Einsweiler (Eds.), *Shared Power: What Is It? How Does It Work? How Can We Make It Better?* (Vol. 4, pp. 77–95). University Press of America.

About the Author

Jennifer Rippner is currently the Executive Director for Policy and Partnerships at the University System of Georgia and the Coordinator of the Georgia Alliance of Education Agency Heads, the state's P-20 council. She most recently served as a postdoctoral research and teaching associate at the Institute of Higher Education at the University of Georgia after completing her doctorate there in 2013.

She started her career as a charter school director in Florida and later became Director of the Florida Charter School Accountability Center, a statewide resource center housed at Florida State University. Rippner then moved to Georgia, where she managed the state's charter school and alternative education programs at the Georgia Department of Education. She then served as Education Policy Advisor to former Georgia Governor Sonny Perdue as well as Executive Director of the Governor's Office of Student Achievement, a statewide P-20 accountability agency where she oversaw the establishment of several education research projects. She also served as a Senior Policy and Legal Advisor at EducationCounsel, LLC, a national education law and policy firm, where she authored several policy briefs regarding access and diversity issues in higher education.

Rippner is a past member of the Southern Regional Education Board and is currently the Chairman of Georgia's State Charter Schools Commission.

She was one of three Americans chosen for a Global Policy Fellowship with the National Institute of Higher Education Policy in 2008.

Her academic research focuses on the role of state education policy and P-20 councils in helping states meet their educational attainment goals. She has presented multiple papers at academic conferences and has had her research on P-20 councils accepted for publication in peer-reviewed academic journals.

Rippner earned a Bachelor of Arts in political science and Juris Doctorate from the University of Florida and a Ph.D. in Higher Education from the University of Georgia.

Index

Note: Italicized page numbers indicate a figure on the corresponding page. Page numbers in bold indicate a table on the corresponding page.